The Modern AEC Marketer

How the Next Generation Will Lead the Industry *Forward*

Judy Sparks

Copyright © 2026 by Judy Sparks

All rights reserved.

No part of this book may be reproduced, distributed, or transmitted in any form or by any means, including photocopying, recording, or other electronic or mechanical methods, without the prior written permission of the publisher, except in the case of brief quotations embodied in critical reviews and certain other noncommercial uses permitted by copyright law.

The information contained in this book is provided for informational and educational purposes only and does not constitute legal, financial, engineering, architectural, or professional advice. The author and publisher disclaim any liability arising from the use or application of the information contained herein.

The views expressed in this book are those of the author and do not necessarily reflect the views of any organization, employer, or client. Examples, case studies, and scenarios are illustrative only and are not guarantees of outcomes or results.

All trademarks referenced in this book are the property of their respective owners. The use of trademarks does not imply endorsement.

ISBN: 979-8-218-91209-3

Printed in the United States of America

First edition

TABLE OF CONTENTS

Foreword 5

Introduction 9

PART I The Mindset Shift 13

Chapter 1 The Beginning 15
Chapter 2 The Time is Now 19
Chapter 3 How We Got Here 21
Chapter 4 The Great Disconnect 25
Chapter 5 The Shift to Full-Funnel Thinking 29
Chapter 6 What Leadership Looks Like Now 37
Chapter 7 Speaking the Language of the C-Suite 41
Chapter 8 Bridging the Gap Between Marketing and Operations ... 47
Chapter 9 Building Trust Across the Firm 51
Chapter 10 From Trusted Advisor to Change Agent 55
Chapter 11 Evolution is What Separates the Leaders 59
Chapter 12 The Courage to Disrupt 63
Chapter 13 The Future is Creative 67
Chapter 14 The Marketer's Mandate 71

PART II THE PLAYBOOK 75

Chapter 15 The Anatomy of a Full-Funnel Strategy 77
Chapter 16 The Scalable 6™ Framework 85
Chapter 17 Account-Based Marketing for AEC 93
Chapter 18 From Proposals to Pipelines 111
Chapter 19 The Art of the Pitch 121
Chapter 20 The Talent Crisis No One Wants to Talk About 131
Chapter 21 What Digital Really Means in AEC (And What It Doesn't) 143
Chapter 22 Visibility is the New Relationship 151
Chapter 23 Content is the Product 157
Chapter 24 A New Generation of Buyers has Arrived 165
Chapter 25 How Millennials and Gen Z Make Decisions 173
Chapter 26 Why "Relationships" Don't Look the Way They Used To 181
Chapter 27 Why Most AEC Firms Struggle with Change 187
Chapter 28 Leadership in a Market That Won't Slow Down 193
Chapter 29 The Invisible Forces That Shape Firm Behavior 199
Chapter 30 The End of Order-Taker Marketing 203

Chapter 31 Thinking Like a CMO (Even If You're Not One Yet) 207
Chapter 32 Separating the Marketing Leaders from Coordinators 213
Chapter 33 Becoming Indispensable in a Firm That's Still Evolving 215
Chapter 34 The Future of AEC Belongs to the Brave 217

Epilogue-Why Your Work Matters 219
Acknowledgements 223
About The Author 227

Foreword

When I first met Judy Sparks, she was a sales specialist focused on the higher education market in a large design/build firm I had just joined. I had practiced as an architect and senior principal in several firms both large and small. Some were pretty sophisticated from a "business development" perspective. Others, not so much. But all were convinced that the seller/doer model and relationship-based marketing was the way to go in AEC, and casting the widest possible net was the secret to generating business.

Judy wasn't buying that. Oh, she believed in forming relationships. But she was laser focused on her market (higher ed), and she was determined to know every single decision maker in that market in the entire southeastern US. She came as close to achieving that goal as anyone I ever knew in our industry. As a result, there was rarely a project in her vertical that she didn't know about well in advance...usually well ahead of the competition. This gave us the opportunity to learn about the projects, pick the ones we wanted, meet the decision makers before the inevitable communication blackout, ask questions about what they were really looking for, and often be the preferred choice before the selection process ever started.

Judy was so effective that, within a few years, she had risen to the role of chief marketing officer while she was still in her thirties.

By that time, Judy had occupied virtually every imaginable role in marketing/business development in at least three entirely different types of AEC organizations. She soaked up experience and gained confidence through all of that, which led her to step out of the corporate environment and start her own consulting practice. I think she saw the flaws in the ways that most AEC firms pursue work, and she knew that she could help them.

Since then, I have consulted with any number of AE practices. Whenever I would find a problem in the marketing area, I always recommended that the principals bring in Smartegies, Judy's firm. I had such confidence in her comprehensive understanding of our industry that I knew she could help (and help a lot) if she could make herself heard.

Not every firm listened. Some folks just don't want to hear the truth. But for those who did, it was often transformational.

Think of it. After having served herself in nearly all BD roles, Judy has had the opportunity to examine hundreds of organizations—architects, AE firms, builders, program managers—and to learn from them while she advised them.

Nothing in this book is magic. There have always been firms that excelled in sales and marketing in our industry. Chip Robert built Robert & Co. into a 1,100 person AE firm before

1945. George Heery led Heery International from a small startup to a 1,000-person multi-discipline form in the period of thirty years. Both of those men were intuitive marketers and somehow understood much of what this book teaches just because they were who they were. When you go back to examine their periods of greatest success, you will find, as I have, that they were naturally doing what Judy teaches here. They understood branding. They listened to their customers (or clients, if you prefer). They designed their firms to respond to what their clients really needed. They focused on delivering what they promised, and what they promised was developed based on their clients' true needs.

What Judy has done here is organize in a comprehensive way what she has learned through her experiences. It is about WHAT WORKS. It is also about really thinking about every aspect of the firm and how each element impacts its success. Although this book is primarily written for marketing professionals, it really should be required reading for everyone in the AE environment. After all, every person in every firm in our industry has an impact on their firm's quality, story, and (as Judy would say) alignment. The knowledge in this book will help us make better firms.

The participants in the AEC industry do important and sometimes noble work. What we do is challenging in the extreme. We work hard, stay very busy, and tend to do things as we always have. If this book gives you an incentive to stop and consider your organization and the role you play in it—and to think about ways you can improve both your firm and your own efforts—it will have done what I think Judy Sparks set out to do when she sat down to write.

Ennis Parker, AIA
Professor of Practice
College of Design
Georgia Institute of Technology

Introduction

I turned fifty a few years ago. And while I didn't wake up with a sudden revelation or some dramatic sense of reinvention, I did wake up with a new kind of clarity—the kind that comes from looking backward long enough to finally see forward. You don't get that in your twenties. You don't really get it in your thirties. And in your forties, you're too busy holding everything together to think about legacy.

But fifty has a way of tapping you on the shoulder and asking a different question: **"What will your work actually mean when you're done?"**

I've spent three decades in the AEC world. Not because I planned to. Not because I set out to build a consulting firm. Not because I had some master strategy for how my career would unfold. I stayed because once I found this industry—or it found me—I realized something most people on the outside never see:

This industry is held together by people who care.

About the work.

About the craft.

About the communities we build.

About the next generation.

And for all its frustration, and all its slow-moving parts, and all the ways it resists change, this industry is full of people who genuinely want to build things that matter.

That includes you.

But here's the part no one really likes to say out loud:

We are entering a new era—and the old rules won't carry us into the next one. The firms that thrive will not be the ones who do what they've always done. They'll be the ones to finally align their brand, strategy, operations, people, and digital presence into a modern system.

And the professionals who lead this next era won't be the ones who wait for permission.

They will be the ones who understand how this industry works and how it needs to work going forward.

That is why I wrote this book.

Not to tell my story. Not to romanticize my journey. But to hand the next generation of AEC leaders the things I had to learn the hard way: the truths, the patterns, the frameworks, the traps, the opportunities, the realities that have shaped this industry for decades—and the shifts that will define its future.

This book is for the people inside AEC firms who are stepping into roles no one prepared them for—the marketers, strategists, seller-doers, and emerging leaders who know the industry is changing and want to be ready for what comes next. This book is mainly for Millennials and Gen Z professionals who are being asked to modernize firms that still operate with habits built twenty years ago, and for Gen X leaders—like me—who recognize that the baton is about to pass, whether the industry is ready or not.

Most importantly, this book is for the person who feels the responsibility of growth sitting on their shoulders but doesn't always feel like they have the authority, language, or tools to shape the strategy. If that's you, I want you to know this: you're not alone, you're not imagining the shift, and you're not underqualified for what's ahead. You're exactly who this industry needs next.

As you move through these chapters, pause occasionally and ask yourself:

Where am I playing too small?

Where am I relying on old rules?

Where am I ready to lead differently?

Your honest answers to those questions will matter more than anything I've written here.

PART I
The Mindset Shift

The world has changed; so must we.

Chapter 1
The Beginning

It was 1993 on the 16th floor of Colony Square, a landmark still standing in midtown Atlanta. I didn't know it at the time, but walking into that office was the beginning of a career I would spend the next thirty years building—in an industry I didn't even know existed at the time.

Back then, my "qualifications" were simple: I knew how to type. And I typed well.

I have my Korean mother to thank for that. Thirteen years of piano lessons didn't turn me into a musician, but it gave me the kind of hand-eye coordination that could out-type anyone in that office. And in the early '90s, that was worth something.

My first job was 8:00 a.m. to 5:00 p.m., $16,900 a year, and my primary responsibility was running the switchboard—answering phones with a smile the callers couldn't see but could somehow hear and feel. My boss was a young baby boomer who appreciated my ability to anticipate what he wanted without making him spell it out. It was very much a "watch, learn, and figure it out" kind of environment—the unofficial leadership style of that era.

In those early days, I never found myself dwelling on my career trajectory. Instead, I adopted an innate belief that my path was mine to carve. Little did I know that I had unwittingly embarked on a thirty-year journey of mastering my craft within this very industry—an industry I had zero expectations of dedicating my life to.

Yet here we are.

It's funny looking back now—none of us starting in the early '90s had a roadmap. We didn't talk about strategy, funnels, or brand positioning. We just worked hard, watched, learned, and figured it out as we went.

If you came up through that same era, you probably know what I mean. There were no marketing playbooks in professional services. No CRMs. No content calendars. You earned trust one phone call, one meeting, one handshake at a time.

But the world we built our careers in is quickly fading. The clients have changed. The way we win work has changed. The expectations of marketing have changed. And if you've been in this business long enough to remember switchboards and fax machines, you're probably feeling the same tension I am—**that quiet realization that what got us here won't get us there.**

I realize now that what I stumbled into became the foundation for an entire generation of AEC marketers—the ones who had to prove, year after year, that marketing even *belonged* in this business. We were the ones to bring structure to chaos, to translate technical speak into human language, and to show that relationships alone weren't enough to win work anymore.

As mentioned in the introduction, I wrote this book primarily for the millennials and Gen Z professionals who are now stepping into leadership roles.

You're living in an era now that's finally ready for marketing to lead. The firms are listening. The data is clear. The C-suite is paying attention. **You don't have to fight the same battles we did just to earn a seat at the table—your job is to own it once you sit down.**

The groundwork has been laid. The industry is primed for change.

This is your time to crush it—to bring creativity, technology, and courage into an industry that's been begging for reinvention for decades.

Chapter 2
The Time is Now
Why the next generation of AEC marketers will redefine the game

You're walking into an industry that's been quietly transforming beneath its own steel-toed boots. For decades, design and construction firms thrived on relationships and reputation—*who* you knew mattered more than *what* your brand stood for. Marketing was considered overhead, not a growth engine.

But something fundamental has shifted. Decision makers are younger. Buyers are digital-first. Data has replaced instinct. And suddenly, the very skill sets that used to make marketers seem "soft"—communication, storytelling, empathy, creativity — are now the most valuable capabilities in the boardroom.

You're not here to make things look pretty. You're here to make things happen.

Your role isn't to chase RFPs or crank out brochures; it's to drive strategy, shape perception, and influence how the firm competes in a world where visibility and value are inseparable.

Marketing in the built environment is evolving from a support function into a growth discipline.

That shift didn't happen by accident—it's the result of years of persistence from people who refused to accept, "We've always done it this way." Marketers who believed that the AEC industry deserved better storytelling, smarter positioning, and stronger brands.

Now, it's your turn to take it further.

The tools are in your hands—automation, analytics, AI, digital engagement, and more channels of influence than we could've dreamed of thirty years ago. But technology alone won't set you apart. What will?

Your ability to connect it all—strategy, story, and substance—to drive real business outcomes.

This book is about that connection. It's about understanding what it really means to market professional services in an era defined by transparency, competition, and change. It's about aligning business development, marketing, and leadership toward a single purpose: growth that matters.

You don't need permission to lead the next chapter of this industry. You just need the courage to do it differently. And if you've ever wondered whether marketing can truly move the needle in design and construction, it can. I've seen it, and I have the privilege of living it daily.

Chapter 3
How We Got Here

Marketing in the AEC industry wasn't born out of strategy. It was born out of necessity.

For most of the twentieth century, business development in design and construction was personal, local, and relationship driven. You didn't need a brand when you had a handshake. If you delivered good work and didn't burn bridges, the phone kept ringing.

The first marketers in the industry weren't hired to shape markets or influence strategy—they were hired to make the firm look more professional. Their job was to type proposals, proofread letters, manage the slide carousel, and make sure the FedEx truck didn't leave without the submittal. That was "marketing."

But beneath the surface, the world was shifting. The rise of large program management, public procurement, and private equity began to change how decisions were made. The buyer became more sophisticated. Procurement became more structured. The process became less about whom you knew and more about how well you told your story.

Then came the internet. Suddenly, your reputation was no longer what you said it was—it was what others could find, share, or say about you online. For most business-savvy firms, the marketing department went from the copy room to the boardroom almost overnight.

And here's the truth most firms still don't like to admit: Marketing became essential not because leadership *believed* in it but because the marketplace *demanded* it.

Clients started evaluating firms long before they ever issued an RFP. They were comparing websites, social proof, project data, and cultural alignment. Firms that understood this early gained a massive advantage. Firms that didn't? They were left wondering why the same relationships weren't enough anymore.

That shift—from reactive support to proactive strategy—is what brought us to this moment. It took thirty years to prove that marketing can drive pipeline, influence buyer perception, and grow market share. But the mindset hasn't caught up everywhere yet. Some firms still treat marketing as the department that "makes things pretty."

And that's where you come in.

Your generation inherits an industry that finally sees marketing as strategic—but it's still fragile progress. You have the chance to turn it from a necessary function into a competitive weapon.

The groundwork is there: brand strategies that align with business plans, digital platforms that reach decision makers directly, and data that tells you where to spend your time. But it's up to you to use it well and elevate the profession even further. To turn marketing from something firms must do into something they *can't win without.*

Chapter 4
The Great Disconnect

For all the progress we've made, most firms are still living in two worlds: the one they say they operate in, and the one they do.

In the first world, marketing is strategic. It's integrated into business planning, client experience, and brand differentiation. It drives visibility, thought leadership, and new opportunities. In this world, the C-suite understands that brand equity drives business equity.

In the second world—the one where too many firms live—marketing is still treated as a service center. Leadership calls it overhead. Business development calls it support. Project managers call it extra work.

And marketers are left in the middle, trying to prove their value with the wrong tools and the wrong metrics.

Here's what that disconnect looks like in practice:
- Websites say one thing, but the firm behaves differently.
- Social media celebrates culture, but the culture doesn't feel celebrated internally.

- Leaders talk about growth, but budgets and accountability don't reflect it.
- Marketing teams build awareness while seller-doers chase opportunities that aren't aligned with the firm's strategy.

The result is predictable. Mixed messages. Wasted energy. Lost credibility.

This is the real problem. Not that firms don't believe in marketing, but that they don't fully understand what marketing is.

Marketing is not promotion.

It's not proposals.

It's not color palettes or collateral.

Marketing is the connective tissue that aligns what a firm says, what it does, and what it delivers—across every touchpoint, inside and out.

When that alignment breaks down, firms start confusing activity with impact. They mistake noise for strategy. They invest in visibility without clarity and wonder why nothing sticks.

And marketers end up fighting uphill battles instead of driving meaningful change.

That's the gap this next generation is stepping into.

You have the skills, tools, and perspective to see what previous models missed. You understand digital behavior, buyer psychology, and the power of authentic storytelling. You know strategy isn't about being louder. It's about being clearer and more consistent.

The firms that close this gap will win.

The firms that don't will keep wondering why their brand refresh didn't move the needle.

Because the truth is this:

Alignment isn't optional anymore. It's the foundation of growth. And until firms align how they think about marketing with how they operate, the disconnect will remain—no matter how many initiatives, campaigns, or proposals they produce.

Chapter 5
The Shift to Full-Funnel Thinking

If the last three decades in AEC marketing were about earning a seat at the table, the next one is about what you do once you're sitting there.

The firms that are thriving today didn't suddenly stumble into better luck or better clients. They started thinking differently about pipelines and connections.

They stopped treating marketing, business development, and operations as separate efforts. They began aligning them under one unified purpose: growth that can be measured, managed, and scaled.

That alignment is what I call **full-funnel thinking**.

Many firms never make a true transition to full-funnel thinking. They begin to understand that marketing and sales are different things. They admit that business development is just a polite way of saying "sales." They agree they need more visibility. They acknowledge that marketing matters, but are unsure how to measure it. They give the marketing team a little more budget.

And yet, when you zoom out, nothing really changes.

Marketing still starts when the RFP hits the inbox.

I've seen this play out hundreds of times, and it usually sounds something like this:

"It just dropped. We need to move fast."

"Who's available to help?"

"Can we reuse something from that other pursuit?"

"Let's just get something out the door."

And just like that, the entire firm shifts into reactive mode.

No matter how much the firm claims strategic marketing is a priority, the systems (or lack thereof) reveal the truth: Marketing is still operating manually at the bottom of the funnel. Everything else is talk.

The Moment That Exposes the Problem

I once worked with a firm that was convinced its win rate problem was a proposal problem. Leadership kept pushing for better graphics, different photos, tighter writing, and more edits from the proposal teams. Despite long hours and precise customization, the results never moved.

The hit rate remained below 30%.

Ouch.

Being on any team that only wins a third of the games they play must take a toll on everyone involved.

So, we stepped back and mapped their primary pursuits over the previous twelve months. We looked beyond proposals and shortlists to focus on the entire buyer journey. We wanted to understand where the first touchpoints occurred and how buyers were nurtured over time.

Here's what we found.

In every pursuit the firm won, the first touch was a business development touch. One person knew one person. The origin of the relationship varied—sometimes a personal introduction through a mutual connection, sometimes a conversation that started at an industry event.

This is not earth-shattering news. Our industry was built on a relationship sales model after all.

What mattered was what happened next.

In the winning pursuits, that first touch was intentionally nurtured all the way through the final decision. When relationships were supported by repetitive, systematic, and multichannel marketing touches, the projects were won.

Those touches took many forms: sponsoring industry events with target-rich audiences, automated monthly emails, inviting prospects to appear on the firm's podcast, paid digital ads that extended those stories to look-alike buyers, middle-funnel content designed to influence decision making, and in-person meetings.

Too often, when we begin working with new clients, we find they are showing up for the first time at the proposal stage. Despite producing beautiful, well-written proposals, they are not losing because their proposals are not strong enough. They're losing because they're late to the competition.

The Uncomfortable Truth

In my opinion, AEC selections are rarely black-and-white. And today, buyers often have preferences and opinions well before procurement releases the RFQ.

Full-funnel thinking exists because of this reality, not because marketing needed a new framework.

When marketing only shows up at the bottom of the funnel, the firm is forced to do something impossible: create trust, credibility, and differentiation under deadline pressure with an audience that already has opinions.

That's not a strategy. That's hope.

What Full-Funnel Thinking Changes

Full-funnel thinking reframes the role of marketing entirely.

It stops treating marketing as a reaction to opportunity and starts treating it as a *system for shaping opportunity.*

Instead of asking, "How do we win this pursuit?" the question becomes, "How do we make sure we're already trusted when the pursuit appears?"

Instead of asking, "How do we get more RFPs?" the question becomes, "How do we influence who gets invited?"

Instead of measuring success by volume of activity, success is measured by momentum. Momentum is the real sign of a healthy funnel. The top of the funnel is about perception, not promotion. Most firms misunderstand the top of the funnel, confusing visibility with activity. Posting project photos. Announcing awards. Sharing internal milestones. None of those are inherently bad. But they don't answer the question buyers are asking at the top of the funnel:

What are you known for, and should I pay attention?

The top of the funnel is where positioning lives. It's where the market begins to associate your firm with specific problems, certain ways of thinking, and certain outcomes. When this is done well, buyers don't need to be convinced later. They already have context. When it's ignored, the firm shows up as interchangeable.

The middle of the funnel is where trust is built quietly and collaboratively. **This is the most neglected part of the funnel in AEC firms, and it's where most opportunities are won.**

The middle of the funnel is the long stretch between awareness and procurement. It's where buyers are forming opinions, gathering insights, and watching which firms consistently show up and are relevant.

This is where thought leadership matters.

This is where account-based strategies matter.

This is where digital presence stops being optional.

And this is where marketing and business development must stop operating independently and start working as a *conversion team*.

When marketing is warming the market and business development is chasing unrelated conversations, the system is inefficient. When they are aligned around the firm's highest value accounts, the same messages, and the same priorities, momentum builds.

That momentum leads buyers to develop a preference for your brand, your firm, your people, and your solutions.

The Bottom of the Funnel Should Feel Like Confirmation, Not Persuasion

By the time a client reaches the bottom of the funnel, the work should feel half done.

The interview should not be the first time they understand how you think.

The proposal should not be the first time they see your value articulated clearly.

The shortlist should not be the first time they recognize your name.

When firms get full-funnel thinking right, the bottom of the funnel becomes less frantic. Teams are more confident. Stories are clearer. Chemistry feels natural because the relationship has already been forming.

This is when pursuit work stops feeling like a deadline and starts feeling like a finish line.

The full funnel is not a marketing model. It's a leadership model. This is the part leaders often miss.

Full-funnel thinking forces discipline. It forces prioritization. It forces firms to stop pretending every opportunity deserves equal attention.

It requires leadership to answer harder questions:

- Who do we want to work with?
- Where do we create the most value?
- What do we want to be known for?
- And are we reinforcing that consistently?

When leadership embraces full-funnel thinking, marketing stops being reactive. Business development stops being scattered. Operations start servicing fewer misaligned clients. The firm stops chasing and starts choosing.

What does this shift demand of marketers? This is where the mandate changes.

If you are a modern AEC marketer, full-funnel thinking means you are no longer just responsible for execution. You are responsible for insight and for driving the process.

You are expected to see patterns before others do. You are expected to integrate brand, visibility, business development, and pursuit strategy into a single system. You are expected to challenge activities that do not serve the funnel.

That is leadership, whether the title reflects it or not.

The firms that thrive over the next decade will not be the ones with the best proposals. They will be the ones who understand that winning work is not a moment. It is a system. And full-funnel thinking is how that system finally starts working.

It forces alignment between the message you put into the market and the experience your team delivers once you're hired. It gives marketing a measurable role in business strategy. It helps business development focus on the right opportunities.

And it gives executives the clarity they've always wanted: a dependable pipeline.

The firms that get this right don't just compete better. They lead differently.

They build brands people trust, teams that collaborate, and cultures that attract the kind of talent every firm is fighting for.

That's where the next generation of marketers comes in. You're not inheriting a marketing department. You're inheriting a growth engine that still needs tuning. The frameworks exist. The technology exists. The opportunity has never been bigger. The only question is this:

Will you see the funnel as a process to manage or as a system to lead?

Chapter 6
What Leadership Looks Like Now

The new era of marketing leadership doesn't come with a title. It comes with perspective.

For years, leadership in the AEC world meant tenure—the person who'd been there the longest, who'd "seen it all." But today, the leaders transforming firms aren't the ones clinging to the old playbook. They're the ones who can see across disciplines, connect patterns, and turn noise into clarity.

Leadership in this business isn't about hierarchy anymore; it's about *influence*.

If you can connect the dots between what your firm *says* and what your clients actually *need*, you're leading.

If you can translate technical expertise into a compelling story that wins work, you're leading.

If you can challenge a pursuit strategy because it doesn't align with the client's priorities—and back it up with data—you're leading.

The best marketers in the industry right now aren't waiting for permission. They're shaping strategy, guiding investment, and earning trust by speaking the language of business, not just marketing.

That's the shift.

The firms that thrive in the next decade will be the ones where marketing leaders act less like in-house creatives and more like CMOs—strategic partners who understand how every decision connects to growth, profitability, and value creation.

That means knowing your numbers—not just engagement rates and click-throughs, but revenue targets, utilization, and backlog. It means understanding the client lifecycle, from attraction to retention, and knowing where the friction points are. It means having the confidence to challenge the status quo—respectfully, but firmly—when you see the strategy isn't working.

Because the truth is, leadership isn't about having the answers. It's about asking better questions:

- What are we solving for?
- Who is our ideal customer, and do we know them?
- How does every marketing dollar tie back to our business goals?
- What are we doing that truly creates value —and what are we doing just because we always have?

The firms that reward this kind of thinking will outpace the ones still managing by "how we've always done it."

The next generation of marketing leaders won't rise because they followed directions; they'll rise because they *redefined the directions*. They'll be the ones who can see both the creative and the commercial sides of the business and bring them together into something cohesive, scalable, and smart.

And here's the secret no one tells you early in your career: Real leadership isn't granted by title. It's earned through trust—and trust comes from delivering insight that helps other people succeed.

That's what leadership looks like now.

I've seen this kind of leadership up close.

One of the best examples comes from Scott Steiding, who spent more than twenty years at Morrison Hershfield before Stantec acquired the firm. As a client, Scott was never afraid to assume leadership in his role—even when it meant stepping into territory others avoided.

I remember a meeting where Scott pointed out something most firms quietly accept: Their hit rate on technical proposals was deplorable.

These were the proposals written by technical teams themselves. Some firms call them fee proposals. Others treat them as administrative paperwork. In many organizations, marketing stays hands off and considers them "not our lane."

Scott didn't.

Instead of complaining about the problem or, even worse, ignoring it, he did the work. He started reading the proposals. Comparing them side by side. What he found was exactly what you'd expect when no one owns the outcome—inconsistencies everywhere. Simple misspellings. Conflicting language. No clear value proposition. No story. No discipline.

Then Scott did the thing leaders do.

He translated the problem into business impact.

In that same meeting, he presented a simple theory: if the firm could increase the win rate on those technical proposals by just 5%, it would add roughly $20 million to the bottom line.

That was an initiative the board could get behind.

And that moment kicked off a firm-wide effort to standardize those proposals—not to make them prettier, but to make them clearer, more consistent, and more aligned with how the firm wanted to compete.

It sounds simple. But it wasn't safe. And it certainly wasn't easy.

Because too many AEC marketers take the easy way out, they label fee proposals, technical proposals, or bids as "not my lane." They defer. They stay in their comfort zone.

That's not leadership. Leadership is seeing where value is leaking, even when it falls outside your formal job description—and having the confidence to step in anyway.

Chapter 7
Speaking the Language of the C-Suite

If you want a real seat at the table, you must speak the language being spoken there.

And in most firms, that language isn't marketing—it's business.

Here's the hard truth: The C-suite doesn't care about impressions, open rates, or social engagement. They care about growth, margin, backlog, pipeline, and cash flow. They care about predictability and performance. When they hear "marketing," they're often listening for one thing—return on investment.

So, if you're still reporting activity—number of posts, campaigns launched, or proposals submitted—you're missing the conversation entirely.

To earn influence at the top, you must reframe your value in business terms.

Marketing is not a cost center; it's a growth engine.

Your job is to help the firm make smarter bets—who to target, what to pursue, and how to position the business to win.

That means moving beyond metrics that make marketers feel good and asking the questions that make leaders pay attention:
- What percentage of revenue comes from our top ten clients—and is that healthy?
- How much of our pipeline is coming from repeat clients versus new relationships?
- How efficiently are we converting pursuits into wins?
- Which market segments deliver the best ROI on our effort?

These are the questions that translate creativity into credibility.

I learned this lesson firsthand earlier in my career when I was doing sales for an international design-build firm.

Every quarter, about a dozen of us from business development would fly into Smyrna, Georgia, for reporting meetings at the company's headquarters. The purpose was simple: justify your existence.

We'd go around the room sharing updates on the pipeline. Who had the most leads? Who had the biggest list? Quarter after quarter, my list was always the shortest. But my win rate was the highest, I spent less money, and I never missed my sales goal.

At first, that didn't seem to matter. Volume was still the currency everyone defaulted to. So, I started pointing out the difference. I showed leadership that, while others were chasing more opportunities, I was winning more of the right ones. Fewer pursuits. Higher close rate. Predictable revenue. When they finally looked at the data side by side, it was apparent.

Then something interesting happened.

Instead of asking me to "build more pipeline," leadership started asking *how* I was deciding what to pursue in the first place. We dissected my process for qualifying opportunities and for prioritizing accounts, and how I avoided chasing work that didn't align.

Not long after that, I was promoted to CMO. And the firm shifted its entire approach.

We moved away from volume-driven selling and adopted a competitive intelligence model—one that focused on targeting the highest-value opportunities and ensuring we won more of them. The result wasn't just better marketing. It was better business.

That experience cemented something I still believe today: when you frame your value in business terms, the conversation changes. And when the conversation changes, so does your influence.

When you start framing your insights this way, you stop being the person who "makes things pretty" and start being the person who helps leadership make decisions. That's when doors open.

But here's the nuance: speaking the language of business doesn't mean abandoning the art of marketing. It means becoming bilingual. You must be fluent in both the story and the strategy. The why and the how much.

That's what earns trust in boardrooms that were never built for marketers.

The moment you can connect your work to the firm's financial goals, the dynamic shifts. Suddenly, you're not asking for budget—you're guiding investment. You're not fighting for a seat—you're shaping the agenda.

And once that happens, you stop being seen as part of the "support team." You become part of the leadership team.

Once I was in the CMO seat, the real work began.

That's when I stopped spending time validating what the company wanted to sell and started digging into what our customers were trying to buy. Not anecdotally. Not based on assumptions. Based on data, patterns, and honest conversations across markets.

What emerged was a gap we hadn't fully acknowledged.

Our clients didn't want fragmented services. They wanted certainty. They wanted fewer handoffs, greater transparency in accountability, and a delivery model that reduced risk. They valued speed, coordination, and outcomes more than internal silos.

That insight changed everything.

It informed a complete rebrand that positioned the firm around its integrated design-build approach—not as a collection of services, but as a one-source delivery model. A clearer promise. A simpler story. One that aligned directly with how our clients defined value.

But it didn't stop at messaging.

That positioning forced operational decisions. It reinforced a firm-wide commitment to sustainability —not as a marketing claim, but as a business value. It influenced how we showed up in the market and how we operated internally, from recycling practices to preferences for sustainability-minded suppliers.

Brand stopped being something we talked about. It became something we lived.

And that's the difference leadership makes once it moves beyond reporting and into responsibility.

The next generation of marketers has a huge advantage here. You already think in systems and analytics. You grew up in a world of dashboards, insights, and instant feedback loops. Use that to your benefit. Learn your firm's P&L. Ask how revenue is tracked. Follow the money—and then show how your work accelerates it.

Because when you can tie storytelling to revenue, alignment to retention, and reputation to recruiting, you're not just a marketer anymore. You're a strategist. And strategists are always invited to the table.

Chapter 8
Bridging the Gap Between Marketing and Operations

Every AEC marketer eventually learns a hard truth: You can't market your way out of a delivery problem.

No matter how sharp your brand looks or how compelling your message sounds, if the firm can't deliver what it promises, the market will figure it out—quickly. And once trust is broken, no campaign can repair it.

That's why the most effective marketers today don't operate in isolation. They work shoulder to shoulder with operations. They understand that marketing's real power isn't persuasion—it's alignment. Alignment between what the firm says, what it sells, and what it delivers.

Historically, marketing and operations have lived on different planets. One is wired for efficiency, risk management, and control. The other is built around storytelling, positioning, and communication. But when those two worlds finally connect, something fundamental shifts:

The brand becomes real. Because a brand isn't a logo or a tagline, it's a promise.

And every project, every client interaction, every schedule met or missed becomes a moment of truth—one that either reinforces that promise or quietly erodes it.

Bridging the gap between marketing and operations isn't about collaboration for the sake of collaboration. It's about creating a closed-loop system that keeps the firm honest.

Here's what that looks like in practice:

- Marketing brings client insight, market intelligence, and positioning strategy into operational planning.
- Operations bring delivery data, lessons learned, and honest client feedback back into marketing strategy.
- Together, they create a feedback loop that ensures the story told externally matches the experience delivered internally.

I see what happens when this loop doesn't exist almost every time we're hired to do branding work.

In nearly every branding initiative we've led, there's a gap between what the firm believes clients value and what their clients tell us they value. Not a subtle difference—a meaningful misalignment.

Our process is designed to surface that gap. We interview internal stakeholders and ask questions like, "What do you think you do better than your competition? Where do you think your competitors outperform you?"

Then we ask the firm's clients the same questions. Almost every time, the answers don't line up.

One example stands out.

We once worked with an interior design firm that was convinced it was losing work because its fees were too high. That belief shaped everything—how they talked about themselves, how they justified discounting, and how they explained losses internally.

But when we interviewed their clients, a very different story emerged.

In the market, this firm wasn't perceived as a high-end design partner. They were seen as a low-cost provider—the "down-and-dirty" option. Competent. Fast. Affordable. Not highly strategic or design-forward.

So, when clients received fees comparable to those of higher-end design firms—firms with much stronger perceived value—they balked.

The firm wasn't losing because its fees were too high relative to competitors. They were losing because their fees were too high relative to the market's valuation.

That disconnect wasn't just a branding problem. It was an operational, positioning, and expectation problem. The firm was delivering one level of service. At the same time, the market expected another, and marketing was left trying to explain away the difference.

That's the cost of misalignment.

When that feedback loop does exist, proposals stop sounding aspirational and start reading like proof. Case studies stop feeling like marketing polish and start functioning as evidence.

And clients, especially the sophisticated ones, can feel the difference immediately.

The firms that get this right don't just win more work. They keep it. They build reputations grounded in consistency and reliability, not just creativity. For today's AEC marketers, this is a real advantage.

You don't see silos the way prior generations did. You see systems. Use that instinct. Sit in on project debriefs. Listen to client close-out meetings. Ask what worked, what didn't, and where expectations drifted from reality. Then bring those insights back into how the firm positions itself.

Because the future of AEC marketing isn't about selling who the firm wants to be. It's about amplifying who the firm can reliably be. And when marketing and operations move in sync, the story doesn't need embellishment. It tells and *sells* itself.

Chapter 9
Building Trust Across the Firm

Before you can build trust in the marketplace, you must build it inside your own firm.

It's one of the hardest lessons every marketer in this industry eventually learns. You can have the best ideas, the smartest strategies, and a PowerPoint deck worthy of a TED Talk—but if your colleagues don't trust your judgment, your ideas will die on the vine.

And in the AEC world, trust isn't granted by job title or creative talent. **It's earned through understanding the business, respecting the work, and helping other people succeed.**

The truth is that most technical professionals didn't grow up working with marketers. Many still don't fully understand what we do—and that's not their fault. For decades, marketing in this industry was synonymous with proposals and presentations. So, when you show up talking about positioning, content strategy, or brand equity, it can sound abstract or even unnecessary to people who live in a world of drawings, specs, and schedules.

That's why your first job as a marketing leader—especially if you're younger or newer—isn't to prove how smart you are. It's to prove that you *get it*. That you understand what keeps your PMs up at night. That you respect what it takes to deliver a project. That you're not here to make their jobs harder, but to make their wins louder.

I learned this lesson firsthand while in-house at the design-build firm.

We were shortlisted for a student housing project at UC San Diego—one of a small group of teams invited to compete. The shortlist came with a $75,000 design stipend, and the presentation requirements were intense. The client wanted a complete concept design.

The challenge was that the needs assessment and program documents were hundreds of pages long, and my technical teams were already stretched thin. Everyone was busy. Everyone was underwater.

So instead of asking for more time or more attention, I looked for a way to make the work easier.

I decided to take on a task no one had asked me to do.

I spent an entire weekend going through those documents. I created a distilled summary of the technical requirements—specifically identifying the "pass/fail" criteria that would make or break the design. There was no ChatGPT back then. This exercise was manual, tedious work. It probably took me ten hours.

But I knew it would save the pursuit team countless hours over the next four weeks. And it did. What stuck with me most wasn't the efficiency. It was the reaction.

I remember Tom, the head of our mechanical engineering division, looking at the document and saying, "You're not the average marketer. Most marketers I know would never think to do this for me."

That moment changed the dynamic between the team and me. I didn't earn trust by talking about strategy or positioning. I earned it by understanding the work, anticipating the pressure, and removing friction where I could. My goal was to help my technical team because when you make their lives easier, you win trust.

When operations see that, everything changes. Suddenly, you're not "marketing"—you're *part of the team*. You're someone who can translate their technical wins into business value, who can help them tell their story, and who can connect their day-to-day grind to the firm's bigger picture.

Here's the reality: In professional services, trust flows laterally before it flows upward. You must earn credibility with peers before you'll ever influence the principals. And the fastest way to do that is by being *useful*.

Offer insights that make their jobs easier. Anticipate what they need before they ask. Be the one who follows through. Do that long enough, and you'll find yourself being invited into conversations you used to have to fight to join.

And when that happens, you'll realize something powerful—internal marketing is every bit as important as external marketing.

Because before you can lead your firm's message to the outside world, you must align the story inside the walls.

The firms that thrive in this new era are the ones where marketing becomes a trusted connector—the team that brings departments together, breaks silos, and translates business strategy into daily action.

That kind of trust doesn't happen overnight. It's earned, repeatedly, in small moments that add up to credibility. But once you have it, you can move mountains.

Because people don't resist marketing ideas—they resist marketers they don't trust. And once they do trust you, they'll follow your lead anywhere.

Chapter 10
From Trusted Advisor to Change Agent

Earning trust is the first step. Earning influence is the next.

Once you've proven that you understand the business and can help others succeed, you'll find yourself invited into bigger conversations—not just about projects, but about people, priorities, and growth. That's where your role begins to evolve from *trusted advisor* to *change agent*.

And make no mistake—this industry needs change agents.

For decades, design and construction firms have operated on legacy models built for a different world. Hierarchies were rigid. Decisions were slow. Marketing was reactive. Business development was siloed.

That model doesn't work anymore. The firms winning today are the ones adapting fastest—flattening communication, embracing data, and aligning their teams around strategy, not hierarchy.

Here's the thing about becoming a change agent: no one gives you permission. You don't wait for a title or an org chart adjustment. You earn the right to lead change by demonstrating that your perspective makes the business better.

I've seen this moment play out in firms more times than I can count.

A leadership team is frustrated. Win rates are soft. Margins are tightening. Everyone agrees something needs to change—but no one agrees on *what*.

The instinct is almost always the same: Do more. Chase more pursuits. Expand into new markets. Add another service line. Increase activity and hope results follow.

And this is where a real change agent shows up.

Because the uncomfortable truth is that more activity is often the problem, not the solution.

In these moments, the hardest recommendation isn't suggesting something new—it's suggesting something stop. Fewer pursuits. Tighter focus. Saying no to work that looks good on paper but doesn't align with strategy, capability, or long-term value.

I've watched rooms go quiet when that idea is put on the table.

Not because it's wrong—but because it challenges deeply held beliefs about growth, effort, and security. It forces leaders to confront the possibility that the firm isn't underperforming because it lacks opportunity, but because it lacks discipline.

Change agents don't bulldoze that moment. They hold it.

They bring data. They connect patterns. They show how focus improves win rates, how alignment improves margins, and how saying no in the short term creates strength in the long term.

Change agents are the ones who:

- Challenge old assumptions—respectfully, but relentlessly.
- Bring new ideas to the table and back them with data.
- Build bridges between departments that rarely talk.
- See trends before leadership does—and help the firm respond before it's too late.

They know how to meet people where they are, translate vision into action, and create momentum that others want to be part of.

And this is where the next generation has the edge. You grew up in a world of constant change. Technology evolves weekly. Markets shift overnight. You're not afraid of disruption —you expect it. That adaptability makes you uniquely qualified to help legacy organizations evolve.

But here's the truth about leading change: it's not about having all the answers. It's about helping people see that change is necessary—and then making it feel safe to take the first step.

You'll meet resistance. You'll hear things like, "We've tried that before," or "Our clients aren't ready for that," or the classic, "That's not how we do things here." Don't get discouraged. Those phrases aren't rejection—they're fear. Fear of failure. Fear of the unknown. Fear of losing what's familiar.

Your job isn't to bulldoze that fear. It's to replace it with clarity, competence, and confidence. To show—not tell—that innovation can coexist with stability. That evolution doesn't mean abandoning what works; it means building on it.

The most powerful change agents aren't loud. They're consistent. They bring *vision and patience*. They know that real transformation doesn't happen in a single meeting—it happens one mindset at a time.

When you can influence how your firm thinks about growth, brand, talent, and opportunity, you're no longer just "doing marketing." You're shaping the business.

And that's the point.

Because this next era of marketing leadership isn't about creating campaigns—it's about building capacity for change.

Chapter 11
Evolution is What Separates the Leaders

For a long time, differentiation in this industry was straightforward.

You competed on technical expertise.

You competed for relationships.

You competed on reputation.

And once upon a time, that was enough.

But here's the reality most firms are uncomfortable admitting: at a certain level, everyone is technically excellent. Everyone has capable teams. Everyone has relationships. Everyone claims to deliver value.

So, when firms look interchangeable on paper, what separates the ones that keep growing from the ones that quietly stall?

It isn't innovation in the flashy sense.

It isn't new technology alone.

And it certainly isn't louder marketing.

It's evolution. Not reinvention. Not chasing trends. Not abandoning what made the firm successful in the first place.

Evolution is the ability to adjust how the firm thinks, decides, and operates as the market changes—while still honoring its core strengths.

The firms pulling ahead today aren't the ones doing radically different work. They're the ones that have evolved how they go to market, how they choose opportunities, how their teams work together, and how leadership makes decisions.

That evolution shows up in subtle but powerful ways:
- Marketing starts shaping opportunities instead of reacting to them.
- Business development becomes more selective and more effective.
- Operations reinforce the brand by delivering on the promise.
- Leadership asks better questions and expects clearer answers.

I've watched this kind of evolution happen up close.

Not long ago, a national design firm hired a new vice president of marketing. She came from a publishing and branding background, which gave her a deep understanding of storytelling, audience, and visibility. But what stood out immediately was what she *didn't* do.

She didn't assume better branding alone would fix the firm's growth challenges. And she didn't mistake activity for impact.

She understood something critical early on. Without visibility into what was working—and data to inform decisions—

the firm would keep doing more marketing without moving the needle.

So instead of starting with campaigns, she started with infrastructure. Within her first eighteen months, she worked closely with the head of sales to build a connected technology ecosystem designed around one clear goal: understanding whether marketing output was driving real business results.

They invested in business intelligence tools, a modern CRM, marketing automation, and supporting platforms that worked together—not as isolated systems but as one integrated engine. An engine built to track how audiences were engaging, what signals they were sending online, and how those signals translated into opportunity.

For the first time, marketing wasn't just creating visibility. It was creating *measurable demand.*

As prospects interacted with content, attended events, or engaged digitally, those behaviors were scored based on intent. That data flowed directly into the CRM. Suddenly, the business development team wasn't starting from cold lists or guesswork. They were opening their dashboards and seeing warm, prioritized opportunities—marketing-qualified leads backed by real behavior.

That shift changed the conversation internally as well. Marketing stopped defending its value. Sales stopped making excuses about the absence of good opportunities. Leadership stopped asking for more activity and started asking better questions about performance and holding parties accountable.

Nothing about that evolution was flashy. It didn't happen overnight. And it wasn't driven by technology for technology's sake.

It happened because one leader understood that growth wouldn't come from louder marketing—it would come from smarter systems, shared accountability, and decisions grounded in data.

That's what evolution looks like inside a modern AEC firm.

Most firms haven't made those shifts. Not because they can't—but because they haven't had to, yet.

And that's why evolution has become the dividing line.

Not between "good" firms and "bad" firms—but between firms that continue to lead and firms that slowly lose relevance without ever realizing it.

Chapter 12
The Courage to Disrupt

Let's be honest. This industry doesn't reward risk-takers. It rewards reliability, predictability, and caution. The built environment is focused on minimizing risk. On most projects, surprises are expensive, stressful, and unwelcome. That mindset makes sense in project delivery. But when it carries over into how firms think about growth, it becomes a liability.

Because the same instinct that protects firms from construction risk often prevents them from questioning systems that are no longer working. That's why challenging the status quo takes courage. Not the loud, rebellious kind. The quieter kind. The kind that shows up with questions instead of ultimatums. The type that notices friction that everyone else has learned to tolerate and decides not to accept it as normal.

I learned this early in my career, watching how firms handled proposals.

In firm after firm, proposal chaos was treated as a given. Impossible timelines. Unclear strategies. Exhausted teams. Marketing was expected to absorb the pressure, work late, and somehow "make it happen." Long nights were worn like a badge of honor. Burnout was normalized. And declining win rates were explained away as bad luck, politics, or price.

The unspoken rule was simple: this is just how the industry works.

But eventually, I realized something uncomfortable. If everyone was exhausted and outcomes weren't improving, maintaining the system wasn't loyalty to the firm. It was complacency.

So, I started asking different questions:
- Why were we only engaging marketing when an RFP hit the inbox?
- Why were pursuit strategies being decided without market context?
- Why were we measuring effort instead of effectiveness?

Those questions didn't always land well. Challenging the proposal process meant challenging habits, power structures, and long-standing assumptions. It would have been far easier to stay quiet and keep producing.

That's when I understood something fundamental about leadership in this industry: challenging the status quo isn't about tearing things down. It's about refusing to protect systems that no longer serve the firm.

Courage, in this context, doesn't look like reckless rebellion. The most effective change agents in AEC aren't loud. They're strategic. They come prepared with data, evidence, and empathy. They don't just point out what's broken; they offer a better way forward.

You earn the right to challenge the status quo by first earning trust. Once people believe you intend to make the firm stronger, not just make your own life easier, they start listening.

And when you get it right, challenge doesn't feel like confrontation. It feels like progress.

It often starts small. Automating a manual process. Rethinking how project stories are captured and shared. Connecting marketing, business development, and operations data to see where effort is producing results. Each improvement chips away at the belief that "this is just how things are done."

Each win builds credibility. And momentum. Eventually, you realize that challenging the status quo isn't a moment. It's a mindset.

It's choosing curiosity over complacency.

It's being willing to speak up even when your voice shakes. It's remembering that every meaningful improvement in this industry—from safety standards to sustainability practices—started with someone questioning an accepted norm.

So don't wait for permission to lead differently. You won't get it. The firms that will define the next decade are being shaped right now by people willing to ask, "Why are we doing it this way? And what would happen if we tried something different?"

Be that person.

Chapter 13
The Future is Creative

When people hear the word *creative*, they tend to picture designers sketching—the artsy side of the industry. But creativity isn't confined to design. It's a way of thinking. A discipline of curiosity. A refusal to accept that what exists today is the best we can do tomorrow.

The future of this industry belongs to creative thinkers—not just those who design beautiful buildings, but those who create better ways to win and do business.

Somewhere along the way, we engineered the risk right out of our imagination. We convinced ourselves that creativity and credibility couldn't coexist. To be taken seriously, we had to stay in line. But the firms that are thriving now are doing the opposite. They're blending creativity with data, storytelling with strategy, and design thinking with business acumen.

Creativity isn't a soft skill. It's a growth skill.

It's what allows you to see possibilities where others see constraints. It's what helps you connect insights across disciplines—architecture, engineering, operations, technology

—and turn them into a story that resonates with real people making real decisions.

In the hands of a modern marketer, creativity isn't about decoration. It's about *transformation*.

I saw this play out clearly during a pursuit for a replacement campus for West Georgia Technical College.

The shortlist included five formidable design firms with deep credentials and strong relationships. On paper, everyone looked the same. Any one of them could have designed a successful campus.

My client, Wakefield Beasley & Associates, before being acquired by NELSON Worldwide, decided to do something different.

Instead of relying solely on assumptions about what this technical college campus should include based on their experience, the team wanted to better understand how these particular students experience campus life. So, we introduced a creative layer into the pursuit that no one else considered: data.

In less than forty-eight hours, we ran an online focus group on Facebook and LinkedIn using paid digital advertising to reach current and former students of West Georgia Technical College. We asked questions about their schedules, how often they were on campus, how long they stayed, and what they struggled with day to day.

What we learned wasn't shocking to anyone who designs technical college facilities. Many students were nontraditional. They commuted. They worked full-time jobs and attended classes a few days a week. Their time on campus came in long stretches, not quick visits. Things like food service, connectivity, study areas, and places to decompress mattered deeply.

None of this was revolutionary. What *was* different was how that insight was used.

While the other firms brought their best ideas to the table—concept plans, renderings, models, and beautiful visuals —this team brought all those things plus something else: a clear understanding of the college's business and its students' lived reality. The data became the backbone of the presentation. It fueled the narrative. It reframed the project from a design competition into a conversation about outcomes.

What stood out was how this team approached the interview. They did something no one else did. They demonstrated curiosity. They showed respect for the end user by going the extra mile to collect data. And they proved they cared more about the college's mission and operations than simply showing design ideas for the new campus.

That creativity—applied to insight, not imagery—won the job.

That's the future of this industry.

Creativity isn't about chasing flashy ideas or shiny tools. It's about solving real problems in smarter ways. It's about using data to inform design, storytelling to influence decision making, and systems thinking to align teams around what matters.

And creativity is contagious. Once people see that thinking differently leads to better outcomes, marketing culture starts to shift. Meetings sound different. Pursuits feel more intentional. The firm becomes more curious, more relevant, and more confident.

The next generation of leaders in this business will be the ones who harness creativity and channel it into action. They'll be comfortable with ambiguity. They'll treat experimentation as a requirement, not a risk. And they'll lead with empathy—because creativity thrives where people feel safe enough to think out loud and take chances.

The built environment has always been about imagining what doesn't yet exist and bringing it to life. It's time for the business side of this industry to do the same. The future isn't just about building better places. It's also about building better firms.

Chapter 14
The Marketer's Mandate

For a long time in this industry, marketing had a very clear role: Make things look good.

That role made sense when growth was driven solely by relationships, reputation, and a steady pipeline of repeat work. But that world is quickly becoming extinct—and so is the version of marketing that came with it.

What's emerging now is something different.

The marketers who are having the most significant impact today aren't just packaging strategy—they're helping shape it. They're influencing which opportunities get pursued, how firms show up in the market, and how leadership thinks about growth.

Not because they demanded that role—but because the business needed it. This is where the profession is heading.

Marketing is no longer operating on the edges of decision-making. When it works, it sits at the intersection of brand, business strategy, operations, and demand. It connects dots that other functions don't always see—between visibility and pipeline, positioning and pursuit strategy, culture and credibility.

That perspective isn't decorative. It's directional.

The marketers who thrive in this environment understand the firm as a system, not a set of departments. They know how backlog affects messaging, how delivery impacts brand, and how buyer behavior reshapes business development. And they're comfortable translating between those worlds.

With that shift comes a different kind of responsibility. Not a mandate handed down—but an expectation that grows as trust is earned. The marketers who move forward are the ones who stay curious about how buyers think, how technology changes behavior, and how buying decisions get made. They're willing to speak up when something doesn't align—not to challenge authority, but to improve outcomes. They understand the business well enough to have credibility, and the people well enough to build influence.

They don't measure success by how much they produce, but by what that work enables—stronger pursuits, better clients, clearer priorities, smarter growth.

And they don't do it alone.

The strongest marketing leaders build bridges—between marketing and BD, operations and leadership, strategy and execution. They know that progress in professional services rarely comes from grand gestures. It comes from consistent alignment.

Here's the quiet truth underneath all of this: Marketing has become one of the few roles positioned to see the whole picture. What you do with that perspective is up to you.

Some will focus solely on execution. Others will step into a broader role—not because they were asked to, but because the business needed someone who could connect strategy to action.

That's not about ambition. It's about relevance.

And as the industry continues to change, the marketers who matter most will be the ones who understand that their real value isn't in what they make—but in what they help make possible.

The Modern AEC Marketer

PART II
THE PLAYBOOK

Turning Ideas into Action

Chapter 15
The Anatomy of a Full-Funnel Strategy
How modern AEC firms build momentum instead of chasing work

If you've spent any time in AEC marketing, you already know this truth: Most firms live at the bottom of the funnel.

The entire system—if you can even call it a system—revolves around the inbox. The RFQ shows up. Everyone panics. Emails fly about who's available. Someone dusts off a project description that hasn't been updated since flip phones were still a thing. Marketing gets two days to turn chaos into something presentable.

Then the leadership team wonders why the win rate is 20 percent.

This is what happens when marketing starts too late. This is what happens when activity is mistaken for strategy. This is what happens when firms believe they're competing in a selection process—when the real competition started long before the RFQ ever arrived.

The fastest-growing firms in this industry understand something the rest do not:

Winning work is not an event. It's a process.

And if you want to lead the market, that process must start at the top of the funnel, not the bottom.

The Funnel Is a System

Let's get one thing out of the way. The funnel you saw in marketing textbooks is outdated. Buyers do not move neatly from awareness to consideration to decision. The real journey looks more like a plate of spaghetti—looping, circling, doubling back, forming opinions before you ever get a chance to speak for yourself.

But the funnel is still the best model we have to explain how influence works. Not the steps buyers take, but the layers where your firm must consistently show up with *clarity, relevance, and purpose.*

A full-funnel strategy gives you three advantages:

1. Visibility at the top **so buyers know you exist**
2. Credibility in the middle, **so they trust what you say**
3. Comparative advantage at the bottom, **so they prefer you when it counts**

Miss any one of these, and you don't have a marketing system. You have disconnected tactics.

Top of the Funnel: Awareness and Positioning

This is where buyers meet you—often years before a project is ever defined.

Top-of-funnel is where reputation forms, whether you're paying attention or not. It's where clients quietly gather signals about who you are and whether you're worth considering.

They're asking themselves questions like:
- What do these people stand for?
- What are they known for?
- Do they understand projects like ours?
- Are they relevant to where we're headed?

What top-of-funnel is not:
- Company picnic photos on LinkedIn
- Project dumps with no narrative
- Websites that sound like everyone else

Top-of-funnel is not about posting. It's about *positioning*.

Positioning forces hard conversations:
- Whom do we serve best?
- What markets matter?
- What do we want to be known for?
- What value do we create that others can't?

This is your opportunity to shape perception before buyers ever meet you. If you don't, they will fill in the blanks themselves.

Middle of the Funnel: Engagement & Trust Building

In AEC, this is where most buyers live for months—sometimes years.

This is where interest becomes curiosity. Where curiosity becomes trust. And where momentum is either built or lost.

The middle of the funnel is the difference between:
- Being shortlisted or quietly forgotten
- A conversation that continues or one that fades
- "Let's stay in touch," and "Let's move forward."

At this stage, your job is simple:

Stay relevant. Stay present. Stay useful.

Not salesy.

Not spammy.

Not chasing attention.

Useful.

This is where thought leadership, Account-Based Marketing (ABM), digital engagement, speaking, and BD alignment must work together. If they operate separately, your funnel leaks. And this is also where brand power shows up in ways most firms don't expect.

A Proof Point: HOK and Mercedes-Benz Stadium

Bill Johnson, Senior Vice President and Design Principal at HOK, shared a story on our *AEC Marketing for Principals* podcast that perfectly illustrates the power of the middle of the funnel.

When the Mercedes-Benz Stadium project in Atlanta was first announced, HOK passed on the opportunity. The firm was busy. Backlog was strong. The cost and risk of competing were significant. On paper, it didn't make sense.

While other firms were forming teams, meeting stakeholders, and positioning themselves, HOK stepped back.

Then something unusual happened.

The owner's advisory team reached out and asked HOK to reconsider. Not because of a relationship built during procurement, but because of *who HOK was known to be*. Their reputation, thought leadership, and credibility in sports and entertainment design gave their absence enough gravity that it was noticeable.

HOK entered the competition late. They were the dark horse. Consultants were already aligned. Politics were already in play.

And yet, they were invited to compete.

That invitation did not come from a proposal. It did not come from an interview. It came from years of visibility, credibility, and leadership that had been built long before the RFQ.

That is middle-of-funnel influence at work.

Bottom of the Funnel: Conversion and Commitment

This is where proposals are reviewed.

Where interviews happen.

Where decisions are finalized.

But most firms misunderstand this stage.

Bottom-of-funnel is not the finish line.

It's the moment the buyer finally reveals their true preferences.

Their decision—emotionally and intuitively—was shaped long before this point.

Bottom-funnel success depends on:
- Storytelling

- Cohesion
- Confidence
- Clarity
- Team chemistry
- Making the client feel understood

Your job is not to explain what you do. It's to articulate what it will feel like to work with you.

Beyond the Funnel: Advocacy and Expansion

Winning the work is not the end of the funnel. It's the beginning of the relationship. This is where delivery either reinforces your brand promise—or breaks it.

Advocacy is created through:
- Project success
- Clear communication
- Trust under pressure
- Ease of doing business
- How problems are handled

Your best future work comes from the work you're doing right now. Retention, expansion, and referrals are not BD miracles. They are delivery outcomes.

The Full-Funnel Formula

Visibility → Engagement → Conversion → Advocacy

If you take nothing else from this chapter, take this:

Marketing is no longer about getting opportunities. It's about creating momentum.

Momentum comes from consistency.

Consistency comes from alignment.

Alignment comes from strategy.

The funnel is not a diagram. It's a discipline. And the marketers who master it will shape the future of this industry.

Chapter 16
The Scalable 6™ Framework
The structure that aligns your firm, drives your strategy, and scales your growth

Before I ever built this framework, I lived inside the kind of marketing machine most firms will never have.

When I was CMO at the international design-build firm, I owned a $5 million annual sales and marketing budget. I managed a twenty-two-person marketing and sales team. I always had three agencies on retainer—one for the website, one for branding, and one for public relations.

On paper, it looked like the ideal setup.

In reality, I spent most of my time explaining the nuances of the design and construction industry to people who didn't live in it. Every agency operated in its own lane. When the PR firm landed a great placement, there was a whole orchestration process just to get that story onto the website. Brand lived in one place. Digital lived in another. Sales materials lived somewhere else entirely.

It worked—but it was heavy, expensive, and fragile.

And it became very clear to me that most firms in this industry could never afford that kind of infrastructure. More importantly, they didn't need it.

When I started Smartegies, I began working with small and mid-sized firms across the built environment. And I noticed something immediately. They didn't come to us asking for *everything*. They came because they needed *something*—a clearer brand, better pursuits, greater visibility, help with recruiting, and stronger sales alignment.

But here's what became obvious very quickly: you couldn't fix any one of those things without impacting the others. Every decision touched multiple parts of the business.

That's where the Scalable 6™ Framework was born.

After fifteen years in-house and nearly twenty years serving more than 300 firms across architecture, engineering, construction, and development, this framework has been tested, refined, and proven with AEC firms of all sizes.

At Smartegies, we believe the Scalable 6™ Framework, paired with a full-funnel approach, is the most effective way for firms to scale and maximize return on their marketing investment—without building bloated infrastructure or chasing disconnected tactics.

Why the Scalable 6™ Framework Exists

The firms that grow intentionally all have one thing in common: alignment.

Their brand, messaging, relationships, digital presence, pursuit strategy, and culture reinforce one another. Nothing works against the strategy. Everything works toward it.

Most firms have pieces of this—but not the system.

They think they have a marketing problem, or a sales problem, or a visibility problem, or a recruiting problem, when what they really have is an *alignment problem.*

I created the Scalable 6™ Framework to solve exactly that.

It organizes everything that drives growth in professional services—brand, story, target customer, digital footprint, pursuit engine, and talent experience—into one integrated model.

One system. One truth.

This framework exists for a simple reason: **Marketing, business development, leadership, and operations cannot scale if they operate under different narratives.**

If you don't have alignment between brand, communications, ABM, digital, sales enablement, and talent, you are not optimizing your marketing investment for ROI. You're fragmenting it.

The Scalable 6™ Framework gives firms something they have never had before: a shared language for how growth works. It replaces guesswork with strategy. It connects the top of the funnel to the bottom. It ensures that every decision—from the website to the shortlist interview to the onboarding experience—reinforces the same promise.

When your strategy is integrated, growth becomes predictable.

Let's walk through the six areas.

1. Brand Strategy

Brand is not design.

Brand is not decoration.

Brand is your market position and promise—the commercial identity that shapes what opportunities come to you, what opportunities you win, and how the market assigns value to your expertise.

Brand strategy answers the most fundamental question every AEC firm must confront:

What space do we want to own in the market, and what do we want to be known for when we're not in the room?

Your position drives:
- Which markets you pursue
- What clients consider you for
- How often you're invited to the table
- How much pricing power you have
- What your pipeline looks like
- How talent perceives you
- Whether leadership decisions reinforce your trajectory or dilute it

Brand is a business strategy expressed through perception. And perception shapes market share.

Firms with strong brands don't chase as many opportunities because they don't have to. Their positioning does the sorting.

When the brand is aligned, the rest of the Scalable 6™ Framework is amplified.

When a brand is confused, the rest is noise.

2. Communications

If the brand sets your position, communications operationalize it.

Communications ensures that everyone in the firm—from principals to project managers—understands the story, reinforces the strategy, and speaks with one voice inside and outside the firm.

Most firms underestimate communications. They think it means newsletters, announcements, or social posts.

Communication is the connective tissue of the full funnel.

- **Top of funnel:** messaging that builds awareness and credibility
- **Middle of funnel:** narratives that nurture trust before a pursuit ever begins
- **Bottom of funnel:** language and themes that create confidence and alignment
- **Beyond the funnel:** internal communication that reinforces culture and delivery

Communication is not a department. It is a discipline.

Without disciplined communication, every other part of the Scalable 6™ Framework fractures.

3. Account-Based Marketing (ABM)

An Account-Based Marketing strategy brings focus to your growth model. It replaces random acts of marketing with intentional, data-informed decisions about who matters most.

In AEC, where one client can represent millions of dollars and relationships last decades, ABM isn't optional. It's rational.

ABM identifies two primary targets:
1. **Highest value customers**
2. **Highest value strangers**

Once you know who matters most, everything else becomes clearer. Your content, digital strategy, BD outreach, and pursuits become more efficient because they are more focused. Most firms try to be everything to everyone. ABM forces you to be exceptional to the right people.

4. Digital Strategy

Digital is not a task.

Digital is your distribution system.

It is how your brand, content, and expertise reach the right audience at the right moment.

In professional services, digital is not about scale—it's about precision.

Digital warms the funnel long before BD makes a call. It turns visibility into familiarity. It turns familiarity into trust.

Digital is now your first impression.

The handshake simply confirms what buyers already believe.

5. Sales Enablement

Sales enablement is where strategy shows up when it matters most, when it's time to close the deal.

It includes proposals, interviews, themes, narratives, and early solutions to the client's project. But it is not just document production. It is also where content gold can be mined.

What you pitch—your approach, differentiators, and problem-solving capabilities—should be visible to the market long before an RFQ ever drops. With the Scalable 6™ Framework, nothing is one-and-done. Once pursuits are completed, everything becomes content inventory that can be repurposed into thought leadership, social media posts, and content offers to warm the top and middle of the funnel.

6. Talent Strategies

Talent is the sixth pillar for a reason. Your people are the delivery mechanism for your brand promise.

Talent strategy connects:
- The brand you promote
- The culture you foster
- The expectations you set
- The careers you build

When aligned, talent becomes your advantage.

When misaligned, culture becomes your liability.

Talent is not separate from marketing. It is marketing. Because clients and recruits are both buying the same thing: your promise.

The Power of the System

The Scalable 6™ Framework is not six things. It is one system with six dimensions.

You cannot pull on one without affecting the others.

Growth is not a department.

Growth is an ecosystem.

And when the ecosystem is aligned, your firm doesn't just grow—it compounds.

Chapter 17
Account-Based Marketing for AEC
Why focus—not volume—is the real driver of growth in AEC

Let me start with something blunt: most firms don't have a marketing problem. They have a focus problem. They spread themselves thin. They chase everything. They say, "Yes," to too much. And then they wonder why nothing sticks and nothing scales.

This tendency is precisely why Account-Based Marketing (ABM) exists.

ABM is not a trend, a buzzword, or another "marketing tactic." It is the most logical, responsible, and frankly grown-up approach to marketing in a relationship-driven, low-volume, high-value industry like AEC. I wish I could say I invented it, but sadly, I did not. We can thank the technology services industry for developing what is now one of the most widely accepted B2B go-to-market strategies for professional service brands.

If you're selling toothpaste, cast a wide net. Create impressions. Hope something converts.

If you're selling professional expertise—if your work requires trust, investment, political capital, and multi-year partnerships—you cannot afford to talk to "everyone." Because *not everyone* is your customer, and your resources are not infinite.

ABM forces you to face that reality.

What ABM Actually Is (and What It Isn't)

ABM is the discipline of dedicating your marketing, business development, and leadership energy and budget to the clients who move the business the MOST— not the ones who simply show up.

It is not software.

It is not automation.

It is not a campaign structure.

And it is not complicated.

It is hard because it requires discipline.

Firms resist ABM for three predictable reasons:

1. **They want everything and therefore get nothing.**
2. **They don't know their numbers.**
3. **They're afraid to admit which clients truly matter—because it forces them to make uncomfortable decisions.**

ABM is where a firm matures. It requires decisions that draw real boundaries, and the clarity you've needed starts the moment you commit.

A Story from the Front Lines

The very first firm that ever hired us to develop an Account-Based Marketing strategy didn't come in asking for ABM.

They came in frustrated.

In my very first conversation with their CEO, he said something I'll never forget: "We spend over a million dollars a year going to trade shows, and we have no leads."

That sentence stopped me cold.

They were a national program management, planning, design, and facilities management firm focused almost exclusively on the criminal justice space. They were visible. They were respected. They were everywhere their industry gathered.

And yet, nothing was converting.

Obviously, with a million-dollar tradeshow spend, they were not lacking effort or exposure. They lacked focus.

So instead of recommending more trade shows, more sponsorships, or more "brand awareness," we stepped back and did the one thing they had never done before: we organized their growth around accounts that mattered.

We started with their *highest-value existing customers:*

- Clients whose contracts were coming up for renewal and were must-wins
- Existing clients where they were only earning a fraction of the available wallet and had room to expand
- Existing IDIQ contracts where they had not maximized the awards from the contracts

Then we looked outward.

We analyzed where criminal justice growth was occurring and aligned it with their service footprint. That led us to define clear ABM micro-clusters:

- A state micro-cluster focused on State Departments of Corrections that were planning major prison renovations or replacements
- A city and county micro-cluster focused on municipalities with populations over 200,000 that were growing at least 10 percent year over year

This wasn't guesswork. It was data.

From there, we did something most firms skip entirely: we got serious about the buyers.

We developed buyer personas for each audience. We understood how selections were made, who influenced them, what political pressures they faced, and what kept them up at night. Not generic personas—real ones grounded in how criminal justice decisions happen.

Only then did we start producing content.

Not random content. Not promotional content. Content designed to resonate with those specific pain points. We built evergreen assets, including a podcast, that allowed the firm to demonstrate credibility long before procurement ever began.

Next, we mapped where those audiences lived—online and offline—and redirected marketing spend accordingly. Instead of "being everywhere," the firm became visible in the places that mattered most. Their brand started showing up consistently, intentionally, and with relevance.

And here's the key part: this didn't happen overnight. ABM is not a quick hit.

But after a full year of operating this way—focused, intentional, aligned—the leadership team shared something that mattered far more than impressions or clicks.

They finally had clarity.

Clarity about who their priorities were.

Clarity about how they were going to market.

Clarity about where to invest—and where to stop wasting money.

And they had results.

In twelve months, the firm added *$9 million to the bottom line*—not by doing more, but by finally doing the right things.

That is the power of ABM.

Not volume.

Not visibility for visibility's sake.

Focus.

Highest-Value Customers: Start With the Truth, Not the Wish List

Whenever I talk to leaders about ABM, I start with the same question: **"Who are the clients that actually move your business?"**

I rarely get a clean answer. I get sectors, familiar names, or the clients paying the bills this year. What I rarely get is clarity—the kind that comes from intention rather than habit.

That is the purpose of ABM: **It forces clarity, focus, and the firm to tell the truth about where its real opportunities lie.**

Most firms *think* they know who their best clients are. In my experience, very few do.

Your favorite clients aren't always your highest-value clients. Your oldest clients aren't always your most strategic clients. Your loudest clients aren't always your most profitable clients.

Business metrics, *not nostalgia*, identify highest-value customers:

- Strategic relevance
- Cultural alignment
- Revenue consistency
- Margin
- Wallet share
- Cross-sell potential
- Cost to serve
- Cost of client acquisition
- Your ability to influence the relationship
- Their ability to recognize and value your expertise
- The kinds of projects they bring
- Where they're headed as an organization

When you evaluate this honestly, two things happen immediately:

1. **You uncover relationships you've been under-invested in.**
2. **You free yourself from clients who drain more than they return.**

Most firms have never done this analysis in any meaningful way. They stay "busy" and assume busy means healthy. It doesn't.

Highest-Value Strangers: The People Who Should Know You, But Don't

Here's the part most firms miss: ABM is not just about who you serve now—it's about who you *should* be serving next.

These are your highest-value strangers.

They are the prospects who fit your business perfectly but have never been introduced to you. They have the right:

- Scale
- Mindset
- Spending patterns
- Portfolio and type of work that motivates staff
- Cultural and operational fit
- Appreciation for your value

And this list cannot be desire driven: **"We'd love to work with them" is not a strategy.**

ABM chooses targets based on: **"We are a strategic match, and the metrics prove it."**

Once you know your highest-value strangers:

- Your BD team focuses on the right targets

- Your content becomes intentional to resonate with those targets
- Your visibility becomes strategically placed where those targets are
- Your digital becomes precisely targeted to the right audiences
- Your pipeline becomes healthier and more predictable

This is how you create demand rather than chase it. **ABM is the heartbeat of the Full-Funnel Model.** ABM sits at the center because it informs everything else.

Once you know who matters most, you know:
- What to say
- Where to show up
- What content to build
- What problems to speak to
- What themes to push
- Where BD should focus
- How digital should behave
- What sales enablement should reinforce at the bottom of the funnel

This is how the Scalable 6™ Framework works:
1. **Brand** tells you how to position.
2. **Communications** tell you how to articulate it—internally and externally.
3. **ABM** tells you where to point it.
4. **Digital** tells you how to distribute it.

5. **Sales** enablement tells you how to win it.
6. **Talent** tells you how to deliver it.

Most firms treat these as isolated functions. We treat them as a system. When ABM sits at the center, the entire funnel aligns—not around all clients, but around the right ones.

What ABM Looks Like in Practice (Real Talk)

It's not glamorous. It's not a shiny dashboard. It's not a logo on a slide.

ABM looks like:
- A short target list (20–40 accounts, not 300)
- Messaging that feels personal because it is
- Digital ads are warming up accounts months before BD reaches out
- Content built specifically for an account's pain points
- Leadership alignment around strategic fit
- Fewer "spray and pray" pursuits
- Healthier pipelines
- Better win rates
- Lower cost of acquisition
- Higher fees because the value is clearer

ABM makes everything work better by eliminating effort that never would have paid off.

The Bottom Line: ABM Forces Clarity, and Clarity Scales

When you know who matters most—and why—the entire firm elevates its discipline

Marketing becomes sharper.

BD becomes more effective.

Digital becomes more targeted.

Sales enablement becomes more persuasive.

Talent becomes more aligned.

Leadership becomes more strategic.

ABM is no longer optional—not for firms that want to grow, stay relevant, or compete in a market where buyers have infinite choices and zero patience for firms that lack direction.

The firms that master ABM will win the next decade. The ones that don't will keep confusing activity with strategy.

And yes, you say "no" more often.

That's one of the most significant benefits.

Firms that know their value make better decisions. Better decisions create healthier pipelines.

ABM gives marketing a strategic seat at the table.

To the Millennials and Gen Z professionals reading this: If you want to be taken seriously—if you want to get out of proposal triage and into real leadership—ABM is your path.

ABM requires:
- critical thinking
- business literacy
- data interpretation
- digital fluency
- strategic influence
- the confidence to challenge outdated habits

This is where you stop being "marketing support" and start being a strategic advisor.

The moment you bring ABM into the room, leaders start asking you questions they've never asked before:
- "Where should we focus next year?"
- "Which clients actually fit our strategy?"
- "How do we grow this account intentionally?"
- "What markets will give us the greatest return?"

That's when you know you've crossed over into real strategic value. Not because you asked for a seat—but because you started asking the right questions.

The Takeaway

ABM isn't complicated. What makes it powerful is the commitment to clarity.

Clarity about who you serve.

Clarity about where you're going.

Clarity about what matters and what doesn't.

When you remove the guesswork, everything becomes easier:
- Your brand sharpens
- Your messaging hit harder
- Your digital becomes intentional
- Your sales enablement aligns
- Your pursuits feel winnable
- Your teams feel more confident

ABM removes chaos. It removes waste. It removes the illusion that "busy" equals "successful."

Most importantly, ABM makes growth intentional—not accidental.

Playbook Tools – Chapter 17

Tool 1: Highest-Value Customer Scorecard
Use this to rank your top 25 clients on a 1–5 scale. Total score drives the list.

Business Value
- Revenue consistency
- Margin quality
- Wallet share potential
- Cross-sell potential
- Cost to serve

Strategic Value
- Market influence and logo value
- Future pipeline strength
- Strategic alignment with firm direction
- Relationship depth and access
- Fit with your differentiators

Behavioral Fit
- Speed of decision making
- Collaboration and trust
- Respect for expertise and fees
- Payment behavior
- Ease of doing business

Output: The top 10 become Tier 1 ABM accounts. The next 15 become Tier 2.

Tool 2: *Market Signal Targeting Map*

This tool helps you identify future ABM targets based on data, not desire.

Instead of starting with company names, start with signals that indicate buying intent.

Step 1: Identify Sector-Specific Market Signals

Look for objective indicators that money, pressure, and decisions are converging.

Examples by sector:

Healthcare
- Net patient revenue
- Capital spending trends
- System growth or consolidation
- Aging facilities or service line expansion

Municipal / Civic
- Population growth thresholds
- Bond referendums or capital improvement plans
- Regulatory pressure or facility compliance issues

Higher Education
- Enrollment trends
- State funding shifts
- Campus modernization or expansion plans

Justice / Public Safety
- Facility overcrowding
- Compliance mandates
- Replacement or renovation planning cycles

Corporate / Commercial Real Estate
- Portfolio expansion, consolidation, or repositioning
- Lease expirations, renewals, or headquarters decisions
- Workplace strategy shifts (hybrid, distributed, consolidation)
- Capital allocation toward efficiency, ESG, or modernization

Mixed-Use / Development
- Land acquisition or entitlement activity
- Changes in zoning, density, or allowable use
- Capital stack readiness or financing milestones
- Anchor tenant commitments or repositioning of existing assets

Industrial / Logistics
- Supply chain shifts or reshoring activity
- Proximity to ports, highways, or distribution hubs
- Automation, efficiency, or throughput pressures
- Expansion tied to e-commerce or manufacturing growth

Hospitality / Entertainment
- Tourism growth or significant event investment
- Brand expansion or reflagging activity
- Asset repositioning or experiential upgrades
- Market pressure to differentiate through amenities

Retail
- Portfolio rationalization or store format evolution

- Mixed-use integration or adaptive reuse opportunities
- Consumer behavior shifts impacting foot traffic
- Capital reinvestment in experience-driven environments

Step 2: Overlay Firm Fit

From that universe, narrow targets based on:
- Alignment with your service offerings
- Geographic or delivery footprint
- Ability to scale delivery without strain
- Experience or adjacent expertise

Step 3: Group Into Micro-Clusters

Instead of one-off targets, organize accounts into clusters such as:
- State agencies
- City and county governments above a certain population threshold
- Health systems within a defined revenue band
- Institutions entering multi-year capital planning cycles

Clusters allow marketing and BD to scale relevance without losing focus.

Step 4: Build Personas and Content Around the Signals

Only after targets are defined do you:
- Build buyer personas
- Identify pain points and decision drivers
- Develop content that speaks to *why* change is happening now
- Map where those audiences live online and offline

Output: A prioritized list of high-probability future buyers, organized by market signal and readiness—not familiarity or brand recognition.

Chapter 18
From Proposals to Pipelines
Why the way most firms pursue work keeps them stuck—and what it looks like when you finally build a system instead of a reaction

Walk into almost any professional services firm and ask about their biggest challenge. Nearly every time, you'll hear some version of the same thing: "We're always chasing something." Or "We're so busy responding that we barely have time to think."

People say it like it's normal. It shouldn't be.

The pursuit cycle inside most AEC firms has become an institutional reflex—automatic, urgent, and all-consuming. Over time, firms build their internal structures around that reflex. Marketing lives in triage mode. BD is always "following up." Leadership struggles to see the business strategically beyond whatever is due next Thursday.

Here's the truth: A firm that runs on proposals will always feel reactive. A firm that runs on pipelines starts to feel intentional.

The difference isn't the volume of opportunities. It's the structure behind how—and why—you pursue them.

When you only focus on proposals, you only see what's right in front of you.

Most firms gradually fall into the proposal trap. It starts with being busy. Busy feels like progress. A full calendar of RFPs looks like momentum, even when it isn't. Activity becomes a stand-in for strategy because it's the fastest way to justify the time and energy being spent.

The problem is that proposal activity is backward-looking.

By the time an RFP hits your inbox, the window for influence is almost closed. Someone shaped the conversation before you arrived. Someone established trust sooner. Someone stayed visible longer. Someone invested in the relationship months—or years—before the pursuit ever opened.

Yet many firms still make decisions based solely on what appears in their inboxes, as if that represents the market. It doesn't. It represents the market's leftovers.

A pipeline, on the other hand, reflects a strategic choice. It tells you not just what you're chasing, but what you're building. It shows direction, not circumstance. And when leadership takes pipeline development seriously, the entire pursuit culture begins to change.

Pipeline thinking is a shift in how the firm sees opportunity.

Pipeline thinking isn't about chasing the next project. It's about shaping demand, so the right opportunities come your way —and being prepared when they do.

It's built on three simple ideas:

1. Not every opportunity deserves your effort.

   This industry has a long-standing fear of saying no. But if you can't say no, you don't have a strategy—you have a reflex.

2. You should know what's coming before it comes.

   Not because someone forwarded a rumor, but because you're intentionally cultivating relationships, tracking market signals, and monitoring the capital plans of clients that matter.

3. Your best future work usually comes from the work you already have.

   Expansion is a pipeline discipline, not a pleasant surprise.

When these ideas are applied consistently, the pursuit calendar starts to look less like a fire drill and more like a roadmap.

The Firms That Win Consistently Prepare Long Before the Pursuit Exists

One reason the pursuit culture stays dysfunctional is that firms pretend every opportunity starts at the same point: the RFP release.

Anyone who has been in this industry long enough knows that isn't true. The RFP isn't where the race begins—it's where it becomes visible.

Most of the real work happens earlier: shaping how clients think about their challenges, reinforcing expertise digitally, staying present during planning cycles, and building familiarity long before competition begins.

The full-funnel model exists because of this reality, not theory. Top- and middle-funnel visibility determine whether the bottom of the funnel is even viable.

When proposals are treated as the beginning of the process, everything feels rushed. When they're treated as part of a larger system, the firm finally gains leverage.

Why Your Pipeline is a Better Indicator of Firm Health Than Your Backlog

Backlog tells you what you've already won.

Pipeline tells you whether that success will continue.

Backlog is a lagging indicator.

Pipeline is a leading indicator.

Backlog tells you nothing about whether:
- the right opportunities are coming
- your business model is shifting
- your brand is resonating
- relationships are deepening
- your pricing power is improving
- you'll be relevant two years from now

If leadership relies solely on backlog to understand the business, they're driving by looking in the rearview mirror.

Pipeline health also exposes issues proposals never will:
- weak differentiation
- inconsistent positioning

- fragmented BD follow-up
- limited visibility
- over-reliance on a single champion
- internal bottlenecks
- sector dependency that's quietly eroding stability

When the pipeline is weak, the root cause is rarely the market. It's almost always internal misalignment.

Pursuit readiness is not a marketing function. It's a leadership function.

This is one of the most misunderstood aspects of business development in AEC.

Marketing can support a pursuit.

Marketing can strengthen it.

Marketing can elevate it.

But marketing cannot fix a pursuit that *leadership wasn't ready for in the first place.*

Pursuit readiness starts with clarity on:

- core markets
- highest-value customers
- highest-value strangers
- your story
- your role in the client's world
- competitive position

If leadership can't articulate these, no proposal team—no matter how talented—can turn that into a compelling story under a deadline.

A strong pipeline gives leadership visibility early enough to position, socialize, and prepare. And when that happens, proposal teams finally get to operate strategically instead of reactively.

The bottom of the funnel is not where the story begins—it's where it's confirmed.

In a healthy pipeline model, the proposal isn't your introduction. It's reinforcement. By the time a client meets your team in an interview, they should already understand your strengths, your point of view, and what it feels like to work with you.

Most firms rely on proposals to make the first impression. That's why the pressure feels so high—they're trying to accomplish in a few pages what should have been built over months or years.

This isn't about volume. It's about consistency.

When digital presence is active, BD is engaged, account strategies are focused, and the brand is aligned, bottom-funnel teams walk into the room with a head start. And when that happens, clients compare solutions—not strangers.

Pipeline-Driven Firms Win Differently

Here's the distinction:

Proposal-driven firms win when things break their way. Pipeline-driven firms win because they've engineered the conditions.

Pipeline-driven firms:
- see opportunities earlier
- prepare earlier
- tailor narratives earlier
- identify decision-makers earlier
- build chemistry earlier
- warm accounts earlier
- challenge assumptions earlier

They don't just compete better. They compete smarter.

Over time, this changes everything: confidence, pricing power, diversification, and the firm's overall stability.

This Shift is Ultimately a Mindset Change

Pipeline thinking isn't a process tweak. It's a philosophy shift.

A pipeline model doesn't eliminate proposals—it puts them in their rightful place.

A proposal becomes:
- a continuation of a relationship
- an expression of positioning
- the culmination of consistent touchpoints
- a reflection of discipline
- confirmation of fit

Instead of a sprint, it becomes a moment in a longer race—one you've been preparing for all along.

That's the point. Pipeline thinking is the antidote to a reactive culture. It's how firms regain control of growth instead of being at the mercy of whatever shows up next.

Playbook Tools – Chapter 18

Tool 1: The Proposal-to-Pipeline Reality Check

Use this to diagnose whether your firm is reactive or intentional.

Have your leadership team answer these questions honestly:
- How many pursuits did we know about 6–12 months before the RFP dropped?
- What percentage of pursuits had existing relationships with decision makers?
- How often did we help shape the conversation before procurement?
- How many proposals were true "must-wins" versus "why not?"
- How often did we say no—intentionally?

If most answers are "we're not sure" or "rarely," you don't have a pipeline. You have a proposal queue.

Output: A shared understanding of whether your firm is building demand—or reacting to it.

Tool 2: The Strategic Go/No-Go Pipeline Filter

Use this before a pursuit ever hits marketing.

Every opportunity must answer *yes* to at least four of these six questions:
- Is this client or project aligned with our highest-value accounts or target strangers?

- Do we understand the client's business problem, not just the scope?
- Do we have early visibility or influence in the buying process?
- Does this opportunity reinforce our positioning and market direction?
- Can we realistically win at the required fee level?
- Will success here strengthen the long-term pipeline, not just short-term revenue?

If it doesn't pass the filter, it's not a pursuit—it's a distraction.

Output: Fewer pursuits. Higher confidence. Better use of time and resources.

Tool 3: The Pipeline Readiness Map

Use this to move opportunities upstream.

For your top 10 future targets, document:
- Known planning or capital cycles
- Key stakeholders and influencers
- Current relationships (or lack thereof)
- Thought leadership or content gaps
- Digital and visibility opportunities
- BD actions needed in the next 90 days

This becomes your *working pipeline map*—not a CRM report, but a strategic planning tool.

Output: Early preparation, clearer roles, and less last-minute chaos when opportunities surface.

Chapter 19
The Art of the Pitch
Why the teams that win interviews aren't always the smartest—they're the ones who understand what the client needs in that moment

If you've ever watched a selection committee work through a shortlist, you know very quickly that interviews aren't technical evaluations. They are people making decisions in the face of uncertainty. They're trying to understand, in a short window of time, which team they can trust with a high-stakes investment and all the responsibility that comes with it.

That's why the pitch matters.

Not as a performance, but as a moment of clarity.

You might have the deepest expertise in the room. You might have done the exact project type fifty times. None of that guarantees anything if you can't help the client feel confident choosing *you* specifically. And this is where many firms — *especially highly technical ones* —unintentionally work against themselves.

They think the interview is about proving competence. It's not. That box is usually checked before you arrive.

The interview is about demonstrating alignment.

Fit.

Understanding.

The ability to take complex information and communicate it in a way that makes people feel at ease.

It's about reading the room. Adapting. Showing that you see the client as a whole—not just as a project.

And that's the part most firms never train for.

Why Interviews Fall Apart—Even When the Team is Qualified

Let me walk you through what usually happens, because if you've sat through enough of these, the pattern becomes painfully clear.

- A team walks in determined to "cover everything."
- Everyone gets a turn.
- Everyone shares their part.
- Everyone fills their allotted time.
- And no one connects to the client in a meaningful way.

By the end, the committee isn't impressed—they're tired. They've been talked at. They've been overloaded with information they don't need. And they're no clearer on who will help them sleep at night over the next eighteen months.

The team did their jobs. They just didn't do the job that mattered. It's not that they weren't smart. It's that they never stepped out of the mindset of "presenting" and into the mindset of "guiding."

Presenting is transactional.

Guiding is relational.

Presenting fills the time.

Guiding fills the confidence gap.

The teams that win know the difference.

Inform, Influence, and Entertain—The Three Things Every Winning Pitch Must Do

When I teach teams how to prepare for interviews, I don't give them a formula—I provide them with a lens. Because interviews vary, but human decision-making doesn't. Every committee needs three things from you, whether they articulate it or not:

1. **Inform:** Give them the information that helps them understand how you think, how you approach problems, and how you will protect their interests. Make sure this aligns with their evaluation criteria, so it's easy for them to reward your points.
2. **Influence:** Frame the narrative. Explain *why* your way makes sense. Help them see the project—and themselves—through your eyes.
3. **Entertain:** Not in the "tell jokes" kind of way.

In the "hold their attention, engage their minds, and make this feel easier than the others" sense.

Entertaining means you respect the client's cognitive load. It means you structure the conversation in a way that feels natural instead of draining. When a team can do all three, the interview moves from "evaluation" to "conversation. And once you're in a conversation, the dynamic shifts. The committee relaxes. They are more open-minded. They ask real questions. They imagine what it would be like to work with you.

That's the moment you start winning.

The Story Isn't About You—and That's the Most Challenging Part For Most Teams

Let me be clear: You are not the hero of the pitch. The client is.

Your job is to show them that you understand their situation—not the generic, surface-level version, but the real one.

The political pressures.

The operational constraints.

The fears they won't say out loud.

The conflicting priorities they're trying to balance.

The unseen influences are shaping their decision.

Most teams skip this part entirely. They go straight into their slides. Their process. Their expertise. Their portfolio.

But when you skip the client's story, you skip the doorway into connection.

The best teams start with the client. They anchor their narrative in the client's reality. And everything they share, every story they tell, every solution they offer, ties back to that.

It's the difference between saying, "We've done this before," and "We understand what's at stake for *you*." One is background. The other is partnership.

Team Chemistry Matters More Than Perfect Content

There's something selection committees pick up on immediately, even when they can't articulate it: whether a team has real chemistry.

I don't mean whether you like each other or socialize outside of work. Chemistry, in this context, is about how you think together, how you listen, how you hand off ideas, how you adapt when the client takes the conversation in a different direction.

A team with chemistry feels cohesive.

A team without it feels like a group of individuals who happen to share a slide deck.

Chemistry doesn't happen by accident. It's built into the preparation—not the rehearsal, but the alignment.

Good teams rehearse. Great teams calibrate.

They sit down and talk about:
- What the client truly cares about
- What are the fundamental decision criteria
- Who should speak to what
- Where the client may push
- What concerns are they likely carrying
- Who leads which moment and why

Chemistry is alignment made visible. And clients can feel it instantly.

Themes Aren't Gimmicks—They're the Backbone of Your Narrative

If there's one thing I wish every team understood, it's that a pitch without a theme is just information arranged in a sequence.

A theme pulls the story together.

It creates cohesion.

It gives the client something to remember when your faces blur together with the other teams they saw that day.

A strong theme answers one question: "What is the idea we want them to carry with them after we leave the room?"

Themes don't have to be clever. They don't have to be cute. They just need to be meaningful and connected to the client's reality.

A good theme makes your content easier to follow. A great theme makes your story undeniable.

The Role of The Next Generation in Elevating the Pitch

If you're a Millennial or Gen Z professional in this industry,

I want you to hear this:

You have an opportunity that the generations before you did not. You understand how attention works. You grew up in a world where storytelling is everywhere. You know how quickly people tune out and how easily they re-engage when something feels real. You notice tone, pacing, body language, authenticity—all the stuff committees respond to subconsciously.

This isn't about age. It's about perspective. And your viewpoint can raise the bar. You can help your teams simplify their message. You can help them make the story more straightforward. You can help them connect the dots for clients who are overloaded with information. You can help them show up as human beings, not as résumés with voice boxes attached.

Your leaders know how to deliver the work. They need your help delivering the message.

The Real Art of the Pitch Is Making the Client Feel Understood

That's it. All the slide design, the talking points, the handoffs—they're supporting details.

The core of a great pitch is: "We get you. We understand what you're navigating. And we will help you make the right decisions along the way."

When a team makes a client feel seen, the trust follows. And in professional services, trust is the currency.

The irony is that the most memorable pitches aren't the ones where a team tries to impress. They're the ones where a team attempted to connect.

When you understand that difference, everything about your interview strategy changes.

Playbook Tools – Chapter 19

The Art of the Pitch

Tool 1: The Interview Intent Brief

Use this before slides, scripts, or rehearsal.

Before anyone opens PowerPoint, the team must answer these questions together:

- What decision is the client trying to make in this interview?
- What risks are they most worried about right now?
- What does success look like for them personally, not just professionally?
- What do they need to feel confident saying yes to us?
- What do we want them to say about us after we leave the room?

Output: A shared understanding of the *moment* the interview represents—not just the agenda.

Tool 2: Inform · Influence · Entertain Audit

Use this to stress-test your content.

For every section of the pitch, ask:

- **Inform:** Does this help the client understand how we think or protect their interests?
- **Influence:** Does this frame the problem or solution in a way that favors our approach?
- **Entertain:** Does this reduce cognitive load and keep them engaged?

If a slide only informs but doesn't influence, it's background. If it informs and influences but drains energy, it needs restructuring. If it entertains without substance, it's noise.

Output: Cleaner content, tighter stories, and fewer slides that exist "just because."

Tool 3: The Client-Centered Story Spine

Use this to keep the pitch from becoming about you.

Every pitch should be built on this simple narrative spine:

- **Their World** – We understand what you're navigating right now.
- **Their Stakes** – Here's what's really at risk if this goes wrong.
- **Their Decisions** – These are the choices you're weighing.
- **Our Role** – This is how we help you make the right ones.
- **Your Future** – This is what success looks like with us.

If the story jumps straight to step four, you've skipped the connection.

Output: A pitch that feels like guidance, not a résumé recital.

Tool 4: Team Chemistry Calibration

Before developing your pitch, align on:

- Who owns which moments—and why
- Where the client may interrupt or redirect
- Who should respond to what kinds of questions
- What each speaker adds that no one else can

Output: A team that feels cohesive instead of choreographed.

Chapter 20
The Talent Crisis No One Wants to Talk About
Why your firm's growth has nothing to do with clients and everything to do with who's left to do the work

If you've been in the AEC industry long enough, you can feel it—something fundamental shifted in the talent landscape, and it's not correcting itself. We're not just short on people. We're missing an entire generation of mid- to senior-level professionals who should be anchoring firms right now. That gap isn't theoretical. It's structural, and it's already affecting your ability to pursue work, deliver it, and grow.

Most leaders talk about this crisis as if it's a matter of "not enough résumés." But that's not the problem. The real issue is that the industry lost a decade of emerging professionals after the 2008 recession, and those individuals never came back. They left the field, changed industries, or never entered AEC in the first place. Today, we're living with the consequences: a thin Gen X bench approaching retirement, Millennials stepping into senior roles earlier than expected, and a smaller Gen Z cohort still learning the ropes.

Every firm feels this pressure, whether they acknowledge it publicly or not. You can see it in the utilization rates, project delays, frantic hiring cycles, burnout, and the increasing dependence on a handful of high performers who end up carrying the weight for everyone else.

The pipeline isn't just thin.

It's broken.

And if firms keep approaching talent the way they always have, they're going to keep getting the same result: not enough people with the right experience to move the business forward.

Traditional Recruiting Models Were Built for a Market That No Longer Exists

Most firms still rely on recruiters, job boards, and their HR departments to find talent. There's nothing wrong with those tools—they just weren't designed for the market we're in.

Recruiters can only chase people who are already open to looking.

Job boards only capture the actively searching. HR can only nurture candidates who show up.

But in AEC, your ideal candidates are unlikely to be actively looking.

They aren't browsing job boards on their lunch break.

They're not updating their résumés.

They're not taking recruiter calls seriously because they get too many.

The people you want the most—the mid-career professionals with 12, 15, 20 years of experience—are already fully employed, already stretched thin, and already being courted by every firm in your market. They're not responding to inbound recruiting channels because they don't have to. They have leverage.

When the market shifts this significantly, relying on traditional recruiting is like trying to fill a deep-water well with a garden hose—the effort is constant, but the level never rises.

Marketing Is No Longer a Support Function in Recruiting—It's the Engine

The only way to reach the talent you want is through the same systems you use to reach your highest-value customers.

The logic is identical:

- You define your *ideal candidate profile* the same way you define your *ideal customer profile*.
- You communicate consistently in the places where your ideal candidates already spend time.
- You build awareness long before there's a job opening.
- You reinforce value over time, not in one moment.
- You create a brand that makes people curious, then interested, then open to a conversation.

This is not a theory. We've done it.

When we geofenced Autodesk's annual conference for one of our engineering clients, we didn't do it to show off a tactic—we did it because the highest concentration of ideal candidates our client was seeking was physically in one place. We pushed a message to them that had nothing to do with "apply now" and everything to do with warming the relationship. It worked because it was intentional, targeted, and executed like a client-facing campaign.

The same thing happened when we helped an Arizona-based civil engineering firm recruit its next CEO. That was a campaign, not a job posting. We used the Scalable 6™ Framework - employer brand positioning, candidate messaging and targeting, digital distribution and advertising—coupled with a funnel approach to guide a highly selective audience toward a decision. We treated recruiting like a pursuit—because that's precisely what it was.

Recruiting is no longer solely HR's job. It is a marketing and brand visibility function, supported by HR.

The People You Want to Hire Need To Know Who You Are Long Before They Consider Leaving Their Job

A career move is not a quick decision. Candidates don't hand over their stability, their team, and their professional identity on impulse. It takes months—sometimes years—for someone to entertain the idea of leaving, even when they're unhappy.

That's why employer brand matters.

Not a slogan.

Not posters in the break room.

Not a list of "core values" posted on the website.

I mean employer brand in the operational sense: How people in the industry perceive your firm's leadership, culture, portfolio, growth trajectory, advancement opportunities, and stability.

A strong employer brand helps you recruit before you need to recruit.

A weak employer brand forces you into panic hiring. And panic hiring is expensive. You pay recruiters more. You settle for less experience. You strain your internal teams. You compromise on fit.

When you scale all that over two, three, or five years, the cost of a passive employer brand becomes staggering.

Firms that invest in employer brand early avoid the churn. They avoid the desperation. And they build pipelines of high-quality candidates who already understand who they are.

Training Is No Longer Optional—It's How You Close a Generational Gap

If the industry is missing an entire decade of mid-career professionals, the only way to fill that void is internally.

You train people up.

You accelerate development.

You identify high-potential staff early.

You build new layers of leadership.

You give your teams clarity, not chaos.

This is where marketing and HR need to work together—not in theory, but in actual day-to-day practice.

Internal communications is not an afterthought. It is the connective tissue between culture, clarity, and retention when marketing takes ownership of internal communications—the storytelling, the consistency, the message discipline—training programs land with more impact.

Professional development becomes more visible.

Career paths become clearer.

Employees understand expectations.

Leaders communicate with alignment instead of improvisation.

And that alignment builds loyalty.

Loyalty builds retention.

Retention stabilizes culture.

A stable culture attracts talent.

This is all part of the same system—whether firms realize it or not.

Every Part of The Scalable 6™ Framework Shows Up in Talent Strategy

When you map the talent crisis against the Scalable 6™ Framework, it becomes evident that marketing's role is not supplemental—it's central.

1. **Brand:** Your employer's reputation is part of your market reputation. Talent and clients see the same signals.
2. **Communications**: Internal + external messaging shape perception, trust, and stability.

3. **ABM:** Ideal candidates require the same level of targeting and intentionality as ideal customers.
4. **Digital:** Paid and organic channels are the only scalable way to reach people who are not actively looking.
5. **Sales Enablement:** The story and the experience matter to candidates, too—recruiting is, in many ways, a sales process.
6. **Talent:** The endpoint of every business decision is people. Without people, nothing scales.

You can't separate these. They move together, or they fall apart together.

The Next Generation Will Inherit This Crisis—and They Are the Ones Who Can Solve It

Millennials and Gen Z are stepping into leadership at the exact moment the talent crisis is peaking. They didn't create this situation, but they're going to have to navigate it.

Here's what they need to understand:

- Talent strategy is now at the heart of business strategy.
- You cannot grow a firm without a visible, compelling employer brand.
- Digital fluency is part of leadership, not a marketing skill.
- Internal communication is cultural infrastructure.

- Recruiting is not about chasing talent—it's about shaping demand.
- You cannot wait for the talent you want. You must influence them long before you need them.

This next generation has an advantage: They already understand how attention works. They know how people receive information, evaluate organizations, and make decisions. They grew up with digital distribution, and they instinctively understand the importance of repetition, storytelling, and visibility.

If they step confidently into this space, they can build the workforce the industry is missing.

The truth the industry must face: AEC does not have a recruiting problem. It has a supply-and-demand problem.

You can't hire people who don't exist. You can only attract them earlier, develop them faster, retain them longer, and build a brand they want to be part of.

Marketing isn't the accessory in that equation. Marketing is the mechanism.

And the firms that understand that—and invest accordingly—will be the ones with the people, the leadership pipeline, and the stability to grow over the next decade.

Playbook Tools - Chapter 20

Solving the Talent Crisis with Strategy, Not Panic

Tool 1: Ideal Candidate Profile (ICP) Builder

Because "we just need people" is not a strategy.

Use this tool to define who you are trying to attract before you begin recruiting.

Experience & Capability
- Years of experience range
- Technical depth required
- Leadership or mentorship expectations
- Markets or project types they've likely touched

Motivation Signals
- What would make this person consider a move?
- What stage of life or career are they in?
- What frustrations are they likely feeling right now?
- What kind of firm would feel like an upgrade?

Fit Indicators
- Cultural alignment (how they like to work)
- Appetite for growth or stability
- Risk tolerance
- Desire for influence or ownership

Output: A clear picture of who you're targeting—not just what role you're filling.

Tool 2: Employer Brand Reality Check

Use this before spending a dollar on recruiting.

Ask these questions honestly:
- What do people outside the firm say we're known for?
- Would someone describe us as stable, growing, innovative, or safe?
- Can an employee articulate our direction without asking leadership?
- Do our website, social channels, and thought leadership reflect how we work?
- Would a passive candidate understand why joining us would be a step forward?

If the external story and internal reality don't match, recruiting will always be harder than it needs to be.

Output: A prioritized list of employer brand gaps to address before launching campaigns.

Tool 3: Passive Talent Funnel Map

Recruiting is not an event. It's a journey.

Map how a passive candidate moves from awareness to conversation:

Awareness
- Where do they see you?
- What signals are you sending digitally?
- Are you visible where they already spend time?

Familiarity
- What content reinforces your credibility?

- How do they learn how you think?
- Who becomes the "face" of your firm to them?

Consideration
- What makes them curious enough to listen?
- What reduces perceived risk?
- What validates the move emotionally and professionally?

Conversation
- Who reaches out?
- What's the first message?
- How is the role positioned as an opportunity, not a vacancy?

Output: A recruiting approach that warms talent long before you need them.

Why These Tools Matter

They reinforce the core argument of this chapter:

You cannot recruit your way out of a structural talent gap. You can only market, develop, and retain your way forward.

These tools help firms:
- Stop panic hiring
- Focus on passive talent instead of job seekers
- Align marketing and HR around one narrative
- Treat recruiting like the high-stakes decision it is
- Build talent pipelines the same way they build client pipelines

Chapter 21
What Digital Really Means in AEC (And What It Doesn't)

If you've been in enough leadership meetings in this industry, you've probably heard some version of: "Digital is important, but our business is still built on relationships."

That statement isn't wrong. It's incomplete.

AEC is a relationship business. It always has been. It always will be.

But what firms are finally starting to understand—and what the next generation already knows—is that relationships now begin in digital spaces long before two people ever meet.

Digital isn't a trend. It's not a buzzword or a department or a set of tools you "adopt" when you have time. Digital is the infrastructure of modern visibility. It shapes perception. It signals credibility.

It influences who your future clients—and future employees—believe you are. Digital is not replacing relationships. Digital is *where relationships begin.*

And that's the shift this industry is still struggling to grasp fully.

Digital Isn't a Tactic—It's a Distribution Channel

Too many firms think of digital as content creation:

"We need more posts."

"We should be on LinkedIn."

"We should update the website."

Those are tasks. Digital is not a list of tasks. Digital is a *distribution engine*. It answers three questions:

1. **Who needs to know we exist?**
2. **Where do they spend their time?**
3. **How do we show up consistently enough to become familiar?**

AEC has historically relied on relational proximity—"being known" through industry circles, networks, conferences, golf tournaments, and introductions.

Today, proximity happens through visibility.

Through repetition.

Through relevance.

If your brand isn't showing up where your ideal customers spend their time, you don't exist to them—not because you lack expertise, but because you lack presence.

Digital Collapses the Gap Between Strangers and Opportunities

Firms used to believe that opportunities came from relationships. Now opportunities come from relevance.

The clients who will hire you in two years are forming impressions of you right now:
- What you publish
- What you talk about
- What your leaders share
- How your brand shows up
- Whether your expertise is visible
- Whether your point of view is differentiated

Digital is where your future opportunities are warming. It's where your highest-value strangers start paying attention. It's where future pursuits begin.

In the old model, "relationship building" required physical presence. In the new model, relationship building requires *digital consistency.*

Not perfection.

Not high production value.

Just presence and clarity repeated over time.

Digital Isn't About Virality—It's About Authority

AEC marketers sometimes feel pressure to match consumer brands in creativity or volume. That's not the goal. You don't need millions of impressions. You need recognition from the *right* people—the ones shaping capital plans, influencing selection committees, or guiding strategic partnerships.

Authority is built through:
- Clear positions
- Useful insights

- Demonstrating how you think
- Telling actual stories from the work
- Making complex problems feel easier to understand

Authority is what makes a client say: "I've seen their content—they really know what they're doing."

By the time the pursuit opens, your firm is no longer a stranger. You're the familiar one. And familiarity is a competitive advantage.

Digital Is Not a Magical Shortcut—It's an Amplifier

Digital won't fix weak positioning. It won't fix internal dysfunction.

It won't fix a non-accountable BD culture.

It won't fix inconsistent leadership.

It won't fix a brand that doesn't know what it stands for.

But when those things *are* aligned, digital amplifies everything.

And here's the part leaders need to understand: You can't "opt out" of digital anymore. Not if you want to grow. The buyers who will run this industry over the next decade aren't waiting for introductions. They're doing their own research. They're vetting firms online. They're watching how you show up.

Digital has already changed the industry. The only question is whether your firm plans to participate in that change.

Playbook Tools - Chapter 21

Making Digital Work Like Infrastructure, Not Noise

These tools reinforce that digital is about *distribution, consistency,* and *relevance,* not volume.

Tool 1: Digital Visibility Map

If your firm isn't visible here, it doesn't exist to your buyers.

List your highest-value customers and highest-value strangers, then map where they spend time.

Online
- LinkedIn (who they follow, not just where they post)
- Industry publications
- Podcasts or webinars they consume
- Professional associations or thought leadership platforms

Offline
- Conferences they attend
- Boards, committees, or civic involvement
- Peer networks and referral ecosystems

Then ask:
- Where are we consistently showing up?
- Where are we invisible?
- Where do competitors have a presence that we don't?

Output: A short list of priority digital channels that deserve investment—and a longer list of things you can stop doing.

Tool 2: Authority Content Filter

Use this before publishing anything.

Before content goes out the door, it should answer at least one of these questions clearly:
- Does this demonstrate how we think, not just what we've done?
- Does this make a complex issue easier for a buyer to understand?
- Does this reinforce what we want to be known for?
- Does this help a decision-maker feel smarter or more confident?

If the answer is no to any of the four, it's filler—not strategy.

Output: Fewer posts. Stronger signals. Higher credibility.

Tool 3: Digital-to-BD Alignment Check

Digital without BD alignment is just noise.

Once per quarter, marketing and BD should answer these questions together:
- What accounts are we actively warming digitally right now?
- What themes are showing up consistently across content and outreach?
- What questions are buyers asking that digital should be answering?
- Where are we reinforcing BD conversations—and where are we undermining them?

Digital should make BD's job easier.

Output: A digital strategy that supports the pipeline, not just visibility.

Chapter 22
Visibility is the New Relationship

There was a time in this industry when relationships were built slowly and predictably. Leaders invested decades building networks they could rely on for opportunities, introductions, and referrals. Gen X and Baby Boomers built their careers on those relationships.

The next generation will not have that luxury.

The industry is changing too fast.

Clients are changing too fast.

Decision-makers are rotating too fast.

Capital is moving too fast.

Projects are being procured too differently.

And the places where relationships used to form—long-term networking cycles, embedded partnerships, "we've known them forever" familiarity—are shrinking.

The new relationship cycle is visibility.

Clients can only trust what they can see. And today, they're seeing you long before they ever meet you in person.

Visibility Builds Trust the Way Relationships Used To

People follow patterns. When they see your firm consistently contributing to the conversation, they begin to assign credibility—not because you told them to, but because familiarity creates trust.

This is how trust forms now:
- They see your team speak publicly
- They read your thought leadership
- They hear your leaders on podcasts
- They see you participate in industry conversations
- They recognize your perspective
- They begin to understand how you think
- They see you as active, relevant, and credible

Visibility replaces the early stages of relationship-building that once happened through lunches, conferences, and repeated in-person interactions.

You're building trust at scale—quietly, consistently, and in the background—long before your BD team ever reaches out.

If People Can't See You, They Can't Consider You

This is the most straightforward truth about modern business development.

You cannot influence a client who isn't aware of you. You cannot be shortlisted by someone who doesn't trust you. You cannot win if you're not visible.

Visibility isn't about ego. It's about access.

The firms growing today aren't doing more work than everyone else. They're simply being seen by the right people earlier and more often.

That's the advantage visibility creates: you show up before you even realize there is a business opportunity.

Visibility Doesn't Require Perfection—It Requires Consistency

Most AEC firms delay showing up because they want to look polished. Perfect messaging. Perfect graphics. Perfect alignment. Perfect approval processes.

Meanwhile, their competitors are already building momentum.

Perfection doesn't scale. Consistency does. If you have ever worked with my team or me, you know we devoutly believe that *repetition builds reputation.*

The market doesn't remember your formatting. They remember your presence.

A consistent presence becomes part of your clients' mental landscape. It conditions them to think of your firm when specific topics come up—long before a pursuit is formalized.

That familiarity matters most at the bottom of the funnel, where decisions are made by consensus and under pressure.

Visibility is positioning in motion. Visibility is a sustained presence that signals to the market: **We're here. We're relevant. And we know what we're doing.**

Playbook Tools - Chapter 22

Turning Visibility into Strategic Advantage

Tool 1: Visibility Reality Check

Are you visible where it matters?

Answer Yes/No honestly:
- Do your ideal clients see your brand at least once a month without you reaching out?
- Do decision-makers recognize your firm's name before an RFQ/RFP is released?
- Can someone unfamiliar with your firm understand what you do best in under 30 seconds online?
- Are your leaders visible beyond project announcements?
- Does your content reflect how you think, not just what you've built?
- Would a buyer say, "I've seen them around," before ever meeting you?

If more than three answers are "No," you don't have a visibility problem—you have an invisibility risk.

Tool 2: Visibility Channel Map

Where relationships begin now

For each audience, identify one primary channel and one secondary channel where visibility should be consistent.

Owners / Developers
- Primary: LinkedIn, industry media, conferences
- Secondary: Podcasts, thought leadership articles

Public Sector Decision-Makers
- Primary: Industry associations, regional events, trade publications
- Secondary: Digital content tied to capital planning, compliance, or funding cycles

Healthcare Leadership
- Primary: Industry news, system-level content, executive thought leadership
- Secondary: Speaking engagements, data-informed insights

Talent (Mid-Career & Senior)
- Primary: LinkedIn, employer brand content
- Secondary: Podcasts, behind-the-scenes leadership visibility

If your visibility isn't showing up in these places *before outreach,* your BD team is working uphill.

Tool 3: Executive Visibility Audit

Are your leaders helping or hurting your visibility?

Score each on a 1–5 scale:
- Clear point of view (not generic opinions)
- Consistent digital presence (monthly minimum)
- Content tied to firm strategy, not ego or personal passion

- Willingness to engage in industry conversations (panels, presentations, etc.)
- Alignment between what they say and what the firm does

A total score under 15 indicates executive visibility is a bottleneck.

Score over 20 = visibility is working for you, even when you're not in the room.

How to Use These Tools

These are not "marketing tasks." They are *leading indicators* of future pipeline health.

Use them:
- During annual planning
- Before launching new markets
- When the pipeline feels unpredictable
- When BD says, "We need more relationships"

Because visibility doesn't replace relationships—it creates them before you ever show up.

Chapter 23
Content is the Product (Even When Your Product is Expertise)

One of the hardest shifts for this industry has been understanding that expertise alone is no longer enough. Expertise must be visible. And the only way to make expertise visible is through content.

In professional services, content is not marketing material. Content is the public expression of your judgment, your experience, and your point of view.

When someone reads your content, watches your video, attends your webinar, or listens to your podcast, they're evaluating the thing you are actually selling: your point of view.

Whether you call it insight, thought leadership, or perspective, content has become a proxy for trust.

Clients want to understand how you think before they trust you with a high-risk project. And in a digital-first world, content is the most transparent window into your mind.

The Industry Still Treats Content Like a Task, Not a Function

Most firms create content reactively:

"We need a post about this award."

"We should announce we won this project."

"Let's write something for Women in Construction Week."

These are announcements. They have their place. But they don't build authority.

Real content does something different. It offers:

- A point of view on the challenges facing your clients
- An explanation of something complex made simple
- A story that illustrates how your expertise shows up in the real world
- A framework or method that positions your team uniquely
- A perspective on where the industry is heading
- A lesson learned from work you've done

Content isn't about being loud. It's about being useful.

Content Fuels the Entire Full-Funnel System

- **Top of funnel:** Content creates awareness. It puts your firm into the right conversations.
- **Middle of funnel:** Content demonstrates expertise. It shows how you think, not just what you've built.
- **Bottom of funnel:** Content reinforces your story. It creates confidence, clarity, and continuity.

Every piece of content your firm produces adds to a growing library of value that compounds over time. And here's the part most firms overlook:

Your bottom-of-funnel content—project approaches, narratives, technical explanations, pursuit strategies—is a gold mine.

With the right systems, AI allows you to turn that material into:

- blog posts
- webinar topics
- thought leadership articles
- social content
- training material
- onboarding guidance
- BD collateral
- pitch positioning

You already produce the content. You just don't repackage it enough. AI and digital allow you to scale it.

The firms leading the next decade will treat content like an asset.

The firms stuck in the past will keep treating content like a checkbox. The firms building momentum will treat content like capital. Because that's what it is. Every idea you release into the market shapes how people think about you:

- Are you relevant?
- Are you insightful?
- Do you have a point of view?

- Do you understand the problems your clients are navigating?
- Do you make complex decisions feel easier?

Content answers those questions long before you ever walk into a room. And by the time the conversation becomes a pursuit, your point of view has already done the work.

Playbook Tools - Chapter 23

Tool 1: The Expertise-to-Content Translator

Use this tool to turn existing expertise into high-value content without starting from scratch.

Start with what already exists:
- Proposal narratives
- Interview talking points
- Project approaches
- Lessons learned from delivery
- Internal frameworks and methods
- Client FAQs and recurring questions

Then translate it using these prompts:
- What problem was the client trying to solve?
- What decision did they struggle with most?
- What trade-offs were considered?
- What would have gone wrong if this decision had been made differently?
- What surprised us about this project?

Output: One proposal section =
- One thought leadership article
- Two–three LinkedIn posts
- One short-form insight for BD follow-up
- One internal training or onboarding asset

This tool shifts content creation from *inventing* to *extracting*.

Tool 2: The Full-Funnel Content Mapping Matrix

Use this to ensure content supports demand, not just visibility.

For each target market or ABM account cluster, map content across the funnel:

Top of Funnel – Awareness
- POV pieces on industry challenges
- Market trend insights
- "How clients are thinking differently about…"

Middle of Funnel – Trust
- Deeper explainers
- Case stories focused on outcomes, not features
- Frameworks that show how you think

Bottom of Funnel – Confidence
- Project narratives
- Interview themes
- Comparative positioning
- "Why our approach works" stories

Rule: If content only exists at the top, you're visible but forgettable. If it only exists at the bottom, you're reactive. Healthy firms have content flowing *up* and *down* the funnel.

Tool 3: The Content ROI Reality Check

Use this tool quarterly to stop content from becoming busywork. Ask these questions of your content library:

- Does this content support a priority market or ABM target?

- Can BD use this in a real conversation?
- Does it demonstrate how we think, not just what we've done?
- Could this influence a buyer *before* procurement begins?
- Is this content reusable across digital, BD, and pursuits?

If the answer is no to most of these: It's noise, not strategy.

If the answer is yes: You're building content capital.

Chapter 24
A New Generation of Buyers has Arrived

Why do people selecting your firm no longer think, work, or decide the way many leaders expect?

If you look closely at the selection committees shaping the future of this industry, you will notice a clear pattern. The titles are familiar: capital planning managers, program directors, deputy city managers, facilities executives, developers, corporate real estate leaders. But the people holding those titles are no longer boomers.

They are millennials.

And increasingly, they are the oldest members of Gen Z.

People in their early thirties to mid-forties are now running procurement cycles, shaping master plans, managing multimillion-dollar capital programs, and influencing which firms get shortlisted. They have authority. They manage budgets. They lead teams. They sign contracts.

This shift did not happen overnight. It happened gradually, quietly, and then all at once became impossible to ignore.

Yet many firms still talk about millennials as "future leaders." They are not next. They are already running the meetings.

The buyer changed before the industry did.

Millennials and Gen Z buyers grew up in a completely different decision-making environment. These buyers did not enter the profession during a time when information was scarce, and relationships were the only currency. They started their careers in a world defined by access.

They grew up with:

- unlimited digital research
- public visibility into vendors and firms
- social platforms shaping professional credibility
- instant communication
- constant exposure to design, technology, and innovation
- the expectation that information should be easy to find
- the ability to evaluate firms without ever calling them

They were not taught to wait for an introduction. They were taught to look it up.

They research before they engage.

They form opinions before they meet you.

They narrow their options long before procurement begins.

This does not make them less relational. It makes them differently relational. They still want relationships. But they want credibility first.

This is the first generation of buyers who do not need you to introduce yourself.

By the time you walk into a room, they already know:

- What your website says about you
- Whether your firm publishes anything meaningful
- How visible your leaders are
- Whether your team participates in industry conversations
- Whether your thinking feels current or dated
- Whether your culture looks healthy
- Whether your expertise is clear or vague
- Whether your content is helpful or self-promotional

Ten years ago, you walked into a room and set the tone for your firm. Now the room has already decided before you arrive.

Your digital footprint is your first impression.
Your visibility is your relationship starter.
Your content is your credibility.

This new buyer is not waiting to be convinced. They are waiting to confirm what they already believe.

If you misunderstand how the buyer has changed, you will misread everything else. Firms that do not internalize this shift tend to misinterpret what is happening around them.

They often misread:
- Why they don't make the short-list
- Why interviews don't convert to contracts
- Why messaging isn't retained
- How digital visibility affects BD outcomes
- Why brand matters earlier

This is not a preference shift. It is a generational identity shift.

And it has consequences. If you are still selling to the buyer like it is 2005, you are going to lose. Not because your firm is not good, but because today's buyers build relationships differently, and most importantly, they prefer not to be sold to.

The firms that win today understand this simple truth: Relationships still matter, but they now begin with visibility.

Playbook Tools – Chapter 24

Tool 1: Buyer Reality Check

Use this before you approve messaging, content, or a pursuit strategy.

Ask yourself honestly:
- Would this make sense to someone under 45?
- Does this help the audience with their pain points in their job?
- Is this different from what our competitors are talking about?
- Would this hold attention if encountered digitally first?
- Does it explain how we think, not just what we do?

If the answer is "no" to more than one, you are still selling to yesterday's buyer.

Output: Messaging that earns trust through clarity and breaks through digital noise.

Tool 2: Visibility Before Outreach Map

This tool forces firms to stop leading with introductions and start leading with presence.

For your top targets, answer:
- Where would this buyer encounter us digitally?
- What would they see first?
- What proof of thinking would they find?
- What content reinforces our expertise?

- What signals credibility without asking for attention?

Then map:
- Content
- Speaking
- Thought leadership
- Social presence
- Media visibility

before BD outreach begins.

Output: A warm market where outreach confirms familiarity instead of creating it.

Tool 3: First Impression Audit

Evaluate your firm the way a millennial buyer does. In under 10 minutes, review:
- Website homepage
- LinkedIn company page
- Leadership LinkedIn profiles
- Recent content
- Google search results

Ask yourself:
- Is our expertise obvious?
- Is our thinking current?
- Do we sound helpful or self-focused?
- Do we show people or hide behind logos?
- Do we look like a firm I would trust today?

If your first impression feels vague, dated, or overly corporate, the buyer never reaches the relationship stage.

Output: Clear gaps in visibility, credibility, and relevance.

Tool 4: Relationship Redefined Framework

Use this to retrain internal teams.

Old belief: Relationships create opportunity.

New reality: Visibility creates relationships. Relationships confirm decisions.

Train seller-doer and BD teams to understand:

1. **Digital presence precedes conversation**
2. **Familiarity precedes trust**
3. **Trust precedes selection**

Output: BD and marketing aligned around modern buyer behavior instead of legacy habits.

Tool 5: "Are We Selling or Helping?" Test

Before any content, pitch, or outreach goes out the door, ask:

- Is this useful to the buyer?
- Does it help them think?
- Does it reduce uncertainty?
- Does it respect their intelligence?
- Does it let them opt in rather than be sold to?

If it feels like selling, you lose them.

If it feels like guidance, you earn credibility.

Output: Messaging that aligns with how Millennials and Gen Z want to engage.

Chapter 25
How Millennials and Gen Z Make Decisions
The psychology, expectations, and patterns driving the next wave of AEC procurement

When you understand how younger buyers make decisions, you know why your firm's entire go-to-market strategy must evolve.

Millennials and Gen Z did not grow up in a world where institutions held all the authority. They grew up in a world where information was distributed, options were visible, opinions were public, and expertise was accessible.

That reality shaped how they evaluate everything, including professional services firms.

They Want Clarity, Not Complexity

Older generations often equated expertise with complexity. The more complicated the explanation, the smarter the expert appeared.

Younger buyers reject this entirely.

They want:

- clear answers

- accessible information
- stories that make sense
- frameworks they can remember
- ideas they can easily share upward

If your message feels complicated, they assume one of two things: You don't understand it well enough, or you're trying to hide something.

Clarity is the new credibility.

They Trust Transparency More Than Pedigree

Millennials and Gen Z watched institutions fail publicly: banks, universities, government agencies, corporations, and media.

Prestige does not impress them the way it impressed previous generations.

They look for:
- honesty
- openness
- proof
- real stories
- lived experience
- consistency
- shared values

You cannot brand your way into their trust. You earn it by repeatedly and visibly showing up.

They Research Independently Long Before They Engage

This is where many Gen X leaders still misread the buyer. Younger buyers do not want your seller-doers or BD team for basic information.

By the time they talk to you, they have already:
- reviewed your website
- scanned your social presence
- evaluated your leadership team
- assessed your culture
- compared you to competitors
- reviewed project examples
- consumed some of your content

They are not starting from zero. They are validating what they already believe.

This flips the traditional sales model. Marketing now does what BD used to do.

BD now enters better-informed conversations.

They Look for Alignment, Not Authority

Younger buyers gravitate toward partners who:
- collaborate easily
- communicate clearly
- bring order to complexity
- understand operational realities
- align with their values
- fit their culture

- listen before solving
- show humility
- adapt quickly

They are not looking for firms to dictate solutions from a pedestal. They are looking for firms that help them think more clearly. The firms that win with this generation are not just the most technical; they are also the most aligned.

Playbook Tools – Chapter 25

This playbook is about changing behavior, not just understanding psychology.

Tool 1: The Clarity Test

Use this before approving any messaging, content, or pitch narrative.

Ask:
- Can this be understood in under 60 seconds?
- Could a non-technical executive repeat this accurately?
- Does it simplify or complicate the client's decision?
- Does it explain *how we think* or just *what we do*?

If it can't be repeated easily, it isn't clear enough.

Output: Messages that build confidence instead of confusion.

Tool 2: Transparency Signal Check

Millennial and Gen Z buyers scan for authenticity fast.

Audit your external presence for:
- real examples instead of generic claims
- named people instead of faceless language
- lessons learned instead of perfect outcomes
- specificity instead of buzzwords

If everything sounds polished and safe, they assume it's curated.

Output: Trust built through honesty, not positioning language.

Tool 3: Self-Service Research Path

Map what a buyer would learn without ever contacting you.
Answer:
- What would they understand after visiting our website?
- What would LinkedIn tell them about our thinking?
- What proof of judgment would they find?
- What questions would still be unanswered?

Your job is not to force a conversation.

Your job is to make independent research rewarding.

Output: Buyers arrive already aligned instead of skeptical.

Tool 4: Alignment Over Authority Framework

Use this when preparing interviews and pursuits.
Instead of asking: "How do we prove we're the expert?"
Ask:
- Where does the client feel uncertainty?
- What decisions feel risky to them?
- What tradeoffs are they navigating?
- Where do they need clarity more than credentials?

Then shape the pitch around your answers.

Output: Conversations that feel collaborative and lead to client value propositions.

Tool 5: The "Would I Trust This?" Gut Check

This tool is especially powerful for younger marketers and BD professionals.

Before something goes out, ask:

Would this help me if I were on the client side?

- Does this respect my intelligence?
- Does this reduce uncertainty?
- Does this feel like guidance or selling?

Millennial and Gen Z buyers can sense posturing immediately.

Output: Messaging that earns trust through usefulness.

Chapter 26
Why "Relationships" Don't Look the Way They Used To
And why that's not a problem—unless you're still selling like it's 1999

One of the most common complaints I hear from senior leaders is: "Younger staff don't build relationships like we used to."

They say it as if something is wrong with the new generation. Nothing is wrong. Relationships simply evolved.

The definition changed.

The medium changed.

The speed changed.

The expectations changed.

The way trust forms has changed.

Young professionals are not less relational. They're relational in a different economy. Relationships used to be built on proximity. Now they're built on presence. Boomers and Gen X built relationships by:

- being physically present
- showing up repeatedly
- attending conferences

- joining committees
- sitting on boards
- grabbing coffee
- playing golf
- being known in the market

That system worked when the industry was smaller, slower, and more stable. Today, the pace of business has outgrown proximity. People move faster. Decision cycles move faster. Industry networks move faster. And digital presence is now the primary form of familiarity.

A relationship starts when someone:
- sees your post
- reads your article
- hears your podcast
- attends your webinar
- learns from your content
- watches your team speak
- sees your work shared
- recognizes your perspective
- remembers your name
- associates you with clarity
- asks ChatGPT

Today, relationships begin digitally and are strengthened in person—not the other way around.

Younger Buyers Don't Owe You a Meeting—You Must Be Worth Meeting

Older generations expected access. Younger generations expect relevance and convenience.

They are not going to give you:
- an hour of their time
- a get-to-know-you call
- a casual lunch
- a coffee meeting

Not if they don't know who you are.

Not if your brand is indistinguishable.

Not if your content doesn't help them.

Not if your messaging is generic.

Not if your firm looks like every other firm.

They give access only to those who already feel familiar and valuable. This isn't disrespect. It's efficiency.

Relationships Still Matter—But They Now Begin Long Before the First Handshake

What used to take months or years of in-person interactions now happens quietly through:
- digital presence
- consistent messaging
- helpful content
- visible expertise
- cultural alignment
- strong employer brand

- clear values
- relevance

By the time your BD team shows up, the relationship has already formed—at least partially.

This is why firms that rely solely on personal networks are starting to fall behind. Their competitors are forming relationships at scale without ever leaving the office.

The Firms That Embrace This Shift Will Outpace the Ones That Don't

This isn't about age. It's about adaptability. The firms that cling to the old model are going to wake up one day and realize their biggest relationships retired—and they didn't build new ones fast enough.

The firms that accept that relationship-building is now a coordinated system—digital + content + brand + BD + leadership visibility—will have more opportunities, more inbound interest, and more influence.

Relationships aren't disappearing. They're multiplying. Digitally first. Then in person. Then in partnership.

Playbook Tools - Chapter 26

Tool 1: Relationship System Audit
Answer yes or no:
- Are we visible to our highest-value strangers weekly?
- Do we publish anything that builds familiarity or trust?
- Are our leaders publicly present, not just privately connected?
- Does our message sound like us, or like every firm?

Output: A clear list of what's missing in your relationship system.

Tool 2: The Familiarity Map
List your top twenty-five targets. For each, answer:
- What are three places they spend time digitally?
- What are three places they spend time offline?
- What would they see if they looked you up today?

Output: A visibility plan built around where relationships start now.

Tool 3: The Worth Meeting Test
Before asking for a meeting, try doing at least one of these:
- Share something useful for their role
- Publish content relevant to their current pressures
- Shown up where they already pay attention

Output: Fewer cold asks. More warm conversations.

Chapter 27
Why Most AEC Firms Struggle with Change
The resistance isn't cultural—it's structural

If you've spent any time trying to implement change inside an AEC firm, you already know how hard it is. Even simple initiatives somehow become complex. Processes stall. Decisions get delayed. Everyone agrees something needs to evolve, yet nothing moves.

It's easy to blame "culture."

But the problem isn't culture.

The problem is structure. Most AEC firms weren't designed for change. They were designed for stability. And the systems that create stability often make it nearly impossible to do anything new.

AEC Firms Were Built on a Professional Services Model Designed in the 1970s

The traditional model rewards:
- utilization
- billable hours

- project delivery
- technical excellence
- risk avoidance
- incremental growth

There's nothing wrong with these goals. They made sense when firms needed predictability more than flexibility. But the industry has changed dramatically. Clients expect more. Competition is global. Markets move quickly. Technology cycles are shorter. Talent expectations have shifted. The buyer is younger.

Yet many firms still operate on a model that assumes nothing will ever change. This creates an inherent tension: You can't run a 2025 practice with a 1995 management model.

Change is Hard When Everyone is Already Overworked

AEC firms run lean. Always have. And firms convince themselves that this is a sign of efficiency, when it's a sign of fragility.

When everyone is fully utilized, there is:
- no bandwidth for innovation
- no mental space for new ideas
- no capacity to experiment
- no room for strategic thinking
- no slack in the system
- no one who owns the implementation

You can't expect people who are already stretched to adopt new systems, learn new tools, or absorb new responsibilities. When firms talk about "change fatigue," what they really mean is "overutilization."

Change requires space. AEC firms rarely have it.

Consensus-Based Decision-Making Slows Everything Down

AEC firms love consensus. It feels collaborative. It feels safe. It feels fair. But consensus is slow, and modern markets aren't patient.

When everything needs committee approval:

- decisions stall
- accountability diffuses
- bold ideas are softened
- innovation becomes incremental
- urgency disappears
- responsibilities get muddled

Consensus protects feelings.

It does not produce momentum.

Leadership must learn the difference.

Change threatens established identities —and that makes it personal.

For many long-tenured professionals, their expertise is their identity. A shift toward digital, brand visibility, full-funnel strategy, or new delivery methods feels like a threat to the role they've played for decades.

This isn't resistance. It's fear. And fear is human.

AEC firms only move forward when leaders acknowledge that resistance is not incompetence—it's vulnerability. The solution isn't to push harder. The solution is to lead differently.

The Firms That Evolve Aren't the Ones with the Best Ideas—They're the Ones with the Clearest Ownership

Change fails when everyone owns it, or no one owns it.

Change succeeds when someone is accountable. Not a committee. Not a task force. A leader.

One person is responsible for the outcome, empowered to make decisions, and supported by the firm's leadership. If your change initiative doesn't have an owner, it will die in a meeting.

Playbook Tools - Chapter 27

Tool 1: Change Owner Charter
For any initiative, document:
- single accountable owner
- decision rights (what they can approve without committee)
- success metrics
- timeline

Output: Change with teeth, not meetings.

Tool 2: Bandwidth Reality Check
Before launching anything new, ask:
- What stops today so this can start?
- Who loses billable time, and how will it be protected?

Output: Change that can be implemented.

Tool 3: Consensus vs. Commitment Test
In meetings, replace "Do we all agree?" with:
- "Who decides?"
- "Who executes?"
- "What happens next week?"

Output: Accountability and momentum instead of circular discussion.

Chapter 28
Leadership in a Market That Won't Slow Down
Why modern leadership requires clarity, not charisma

For decades, leadership in AEC was defined by experience, tenure, technical expertise, and steady decision-making. The role was to maintain order, protect the firm, keep clients happy, and deliver consistently.

Today's leaders face a different world:
- Markets are volatile.
- Technology is disruptive.
- Clients have higher expectations.
- Talent is harder to find.
- Generational shifts are reshaping values.
- Competition is broader.
- Visibility matters.
- Pace matters.
- And the industry is no longer insulated from change.

This is the first era where being a steady hand is not enough. Leadership now requires clarity, adaptability, and communication.

Your Team Doesn't Need You to Know Everything— They Need You to Say What Matters

Younger professionals don't want leaders who pretend to have all the answers. They want leaders who can articulate:

- Where the firm is going
- What are the priorities
- Why are decisions being made
- How can they contribute
- What success looks like
- What's changing and why
- What's not changing and why

This is clarity, not certainty.

And clarity is what keeps teams engaged during volatility.

Speed matters more than perfection.

The pace of business used to give leaders months to make decisions. Today, weeks feel long. Opportunities move quickly. Clients expect responsiveness. Talent expects communication. Digital cycles turn constantly.

If you wait for perfect information *(I'm looking at you, architects, who are still selecting which picture to put in the book),* you will always move too slowly.

Modern leadership means:

- making informed decisions fast
- adjusting when needed
- communicating proactively

- testing small ideas instead of launching significant initiatives
- accepting that imperfection is part of innovation

Leaders who wait for the perfect timing are quietly being outpaced by those who act early and iterate.

Visibility is Part of Leadership Now

This is the part many traditional leaders resist.

Visibility is not about ego. Visibility is not self-promotion. Visibility is not vanity. Visibility is leadership.

Your people need to see you. Your clients need to hear from you. Your market needs to understand your direction. Your candidates need to know what you stand for. If your leaders are invisible, your firm is invisible.

Younger buyers don't want faceless firms. They want human leadership—people with a point of view, a voice, a presence, and a sense of responsibility to the industry.

Leadership is no longer just internal. It's external, distributed, and visible.

If You're Not Building Leaders At Every Level, You're Weakening The Firm

Every firm has senior leaders. But the firms that thrive develop:

- mid-level leaders
- technical leaders
- thought leaders

- BD leaders
- practice leaders
- culture leaders
- digital leaders
- brand ambassadors

Leadership is not a hierarchy. It's a team sport. And the firms with the most leadership capacity win.

Playbook Tools - Chapter 28

Tool 1: Speed Decision Rule
- For reversible decisions, decide fast.
- For decisions that are not: slow down.

Output: Fewer stalled initiatives and fewer over-engineered decisions.

Tool 2: Leadership Visibility Plan

Each senior leader commits to:
- one public message per month (insight, POV, lesson learned)
- one internal message per month (direction, priorities, recognition)

Output: Leadership that is seen and trusted.

Chapter 29
The Invisible Forces That Shape Firm Behavior
Why firms act the way they do—even when they know they shouldn't

You can't change what you don't understand. And one of the biggest obstacles to meaningful evolution in this industry is that firms rarely examine the invisible forces that influence their behavior.

People assume firms act on logic. They don't. They act on incentives, habits, unspoken rules, and generational memory.

If you want to change a firm, you must understand what's quietly driving it.

Invisible Force #1: The Pressure to Stay Billable

In a billable-hour economy, time is a currency. And when every hour has a price, non-billable activity feels like a loss.

This mindset shapes behavior:
- Innovation becomes a luxury
- BD becomes episodic
- Marketing becomes reactive
- Training gets deferred

- Internal improvements stall
- Change feels expensive

The firm doesn't mean to resist innovation—it just sees the cost of time before the value of change.

Invisible Force #2: The Weight of Legacy

Firms inherit habits from the leaders who built them. Those habits can be productive or limiting.

Common legacy habits:

"We've always done it this way."

"Our clients don't care about that."

"We know our market better than anyone."

"Relationships will carry us."

"Our work speaks for itself."

Legacy isn't bad. But it can blind a firm to what's happening. The market is not obligated to honor your history.

Invisible Force #3: The Myth of the Hero Leader

AEC firms often rely on one or two individuals who carry the business:

- They bring in the work
- They maintain client relationships
- They shape strategy
- They control key decisions
- They mentor future leaders
- They carry institutional knowledge

When everything revolves around one leader, the firm appears stable—until that leader retires, burns out, or becomes stretched too thin. A firm built around one hero is not a firm. It's a dependency.

Invisible Force #4: The Fear of Specialization

Many firms resist choosing a point of view because they fear limiting their opportunities. They believe broad positioning gives them more access to work.

Broad positioning creates:
- weaker messaging
- unfocused BD activity
- diluted visibility
- generic proposals
- unpredictable pipelines
- low differentiation

Specialization doesn't reduce opportunity. It clarifies it. And clarity is what younger buyers respond to.

Invisible Force #5: The Underestimation of Culture

Firms say culture matters. They rarely treat it like a business driver.

Culture influences:
- retention
- leadership development
- client experience
- quality

- innovation
- reputation
- recruiting
- collaboration

Culture is not an HR initiative. It is the firm's behavioral operating system.

When culture is unclear, behavior is inconsistent. When behavior is erratic, performance is unpredictable. And unpredictable firms struggle to grow.

Chapter 30
The End of Order-Taker Marketing
Why the future belongs to marketers who think, not just execute

Every industry has its stereotypes, and ours is no different. For decades, AEC marketing was defined by proposal production, résumé updates, project sheets, photos, tradeshow booths, and whatever internal teams requested at the last minute.

None of this was strategy. It was administrative survival.

And marketers were expected to simply "get it done." But that model is collapsing—not because marketing teams decided they want more influence, but because the industry itself is undergoing shifts so significant that firms can no longer compete on execution alone.

Today's market requires marketers who can:
- interpret the business environment
- understand buyer psychology
- identify strategic opportunities
- bring data into leadership conversations
- build campaigns that influence revenue

- connect brand to pipeline
- understand the talent market
- drive digital strategy
- shape perception
- help leaders make informed decisions

The modern firm won't survive without strategic marketers. And the modern marketer won't survive by being anything less than that.

Execution is no longer enough—firms need direction.

Leaders increasingly expect marketing to provide:
- insights
- recommendations
- clarity
- structure
- prioritization
- narrative alignment
- competitive intelligence
- visibility strategy

They need someone who sees the bigger picture—someone who can speak to the "why," not just deliver the "what." Marketing is not a service line. It's a strategic function. Order-takers wait for direction. Strategic marketers create the roadmap.

You don't get a seat at the table by asking—you get it by contributing something no one else has.

Here is the truth: No leader is going to "invite" you into strategic conversations out of generosity. They will involve you when they need you. You become indispensable when:

- You see things they don't see
- You bring information they don't have
- You solve problems that they don't know how to solve
- You connect dots across the Scalable 6™ Framework
- You translate market behavior into firm action
- You help them avoid risk
- You help them grow revenue
- You help them make better decisions

That's when you stop being an order-taker and start being a partner. The shift is not granted. It is earned.

Playbook Tools - Chapter 30

Tool 1: From Request to Recommendation Script
When asked for a tactic, respond with:
- What problem are we solving
- What metric matters
- What we recommend and why

Output: You shift from support to strategy in real time.

Tool 2: Impact Tracker
Track marketing output in business terms:
- win rate influence
- pipeline velocity
- target account engagement

Output: Evidence that marketing is revenue infrastructure.

Chapter 31
Thinking Like a CMO (Even If You're Not One Yet)
How influence grows by thinking in systems, not tasks

Becoming a modern marketer in AEC starts long before you have "Chief" or "VP" in your title. It begins with how you think about the firm, the market, your role, and the business itself.

If you want to think like a CMO, you must stop thinking like a coordinator. Coordinators think in terms of tasks. CMOs think in systems.

Tasks answer, "What needs to be done?"

Systems answer, "What needs to change so the firm can grow?"

The strongest marketers make this transition early—long before the title ever catches up.

A CMO Mindset is Rooted in Business, Not Marketing

Marketing strategy does not exist in a vacuum. It must respond to business reality.

If you want real influence, you need to understand:

- how the firm makes money

- revenue mix and margin pressure
- backlog versus pipeline health
- sector performance and exposure
- utilization and delivery risk
- hiring gaps and talent constraints
- cost of pursuit and cost of sales
- competitive positioning
- leadership bandwidth

When your decisions are based solely on marketing inputs, your work will always feel misaligned. When your thinking is grounded in the business, your value becomes impossible to ignore.

CMOs speak the language of the firm—not just the language of marketing.

CMOs Anticipate Needs—They Don't Wait For Them

The difference between tactical and strategic marketing lies in timing.

Tactical marketing waits.

Strategic marketing foresees.

CMO-level thinkers are constantly scanning:
- shifts in buyer behavior
- talent shortages
- emerging competitors
- market and economic signals
- capital movement
- generational dynamics

- digital patterns
- cultural change

When you spot patterns early, your recommendations become proactive rather than reactive. That is how influence grows.

Leaders don't need more execution. They need earlier insight.

CMOs Build Alignment Across the Firm

Marketing, BD, operations, HR, and leadership cannot operate independently in a modern AEC firm.

A CMO-level thinker ensures:
- messaging matches positioning
- positioning reflects market reality
- BD activity aligns with the pipeline strategy
- digital presence supports visibility goals
- talent efforts reflect culture and brand
- proposals reinforce strategic priorities

When these elements align, the firm feels coherent. When they don't, everything feels fragmented.

Alignment reduces friction.

Misalignment creates chaos.

A CMO mindset is ultimately an *alignment mindset*.

Influence Comes Before Authority

You don't get a seat at the table by asking for one. You get it by contributing something no one else is bringing.

Influence grows when you:
- see patterns leadership hasn't named yet
- connect dots across the business
- translate market behavior into firm action
- surface risk before it becomes visible
- help leaders make better decisions, faster

The shift is not granted.

It is earned.

And the marketers who learn to think this way early are the ones who move from execution to leadership—regardless of title.

Playbook Tools - Chapter 31

Tool 1: Business Fluency Checklist

If you can't clearly explain these, learn them:
- how the firm makes money
- what drives margin
- which sectors are growing or shrinking
- how the win rate affects revenue
- where delivery risk lives

Output: You start speaking executive.

Tool 2: Monthly Market Scan

Once a month, bring leadership:
- Three new buyer signals
- Two competitor moves
- One emerging risk or opportunity

Output: You become proactive instead of reactive.

Tool 3: Alignment Gut Check

Before launching any initiative, ask:
- Does this support our priority sectors?
- Does it reinforce our positioning?
- Does it help BD pursue the right work?
- Does it make the firm more visible where it matters?
- Does it align with how we want to grow?

Output: Fewer disconnected efforts. More strategic momentum.

Chapter 32
Separating the Marketing Leaders from Coordinators
What modern AEC marketers need to know

The next generation of AEC marketers doesn't need more templates. They need training. These are the skills that matter now:

Business Literacy

You must understand how the firm operates financially: revenue mix, margins, utilization, pipeline, and cost of sales. Without this, you cannot influence decisions.

Messaging and Narrative Development

Modern marketers simplify complexity. They articulate points of view, build themes, frame value, and create stories that resonate with buyers and committees.

This is not copywriting.

It is strategic communication.

Digital Strategy and Distribution

Visibility is powered by digital infrastructure. You must understand paid and organic channels, targeting, retargeting, funnels, analytics, and content distribution. Digital is the engine of relevance.

ABM and Pipeline Strategy

ABM is no longer optional. It requires prioritization, account scoring, relationship mapping, and aligned content. Marketers must own part of this system.

Internal Communications

Internal clarity drives retention. Marketers who can translate strategy, reinforce culture, prepare leaders to communicate change, and stabilize teams are invaluable.

Pitch and Presentation Strategy

Winning interviews requires narrative design, theme development, rehearsal discipline, and psychological awareness. This is persuasion engineering.

Leadership and Influence

Leadership is not a title. It is confidence, clarity, self-awareness, curiosity, and the willingness to speak truth when it matters.

These skills don't make you busy. They make you valuable.

Chapter 33
Becoming Indispensable in a Firm That's Still Evolving
How careers grow alongside industry change

AEC firms are evolving at different speeds. Some move fast. Some inch forward. Some resist entirely. But you can thrive in any environment if you understand what makes someone indispensable.

Indispensable marketers solve real business problems. They help firms:

- win more strategically
- communicate more clearly
- differentiate meaningfully
- attract and retain talent
- stabilize culture
- anticipate market shifts
- reduce chaos
- align teams

They see patterns that leadership misses because leadership is buried in delivery, risk, staffing, and operations.

They also build cross-functional trust. Influence requires credibility with marketing, BD, technical teams, HR, operations, finance, and leadership. This is not manipulation. It is political intelligence.

Indispensable marketers do not wait for permission. They initiate, propose, experiment, educate, and connect strategy to execution.

Leadership is claimed through action, not granted through titles.

The modern marketer is becoming:
- a strategist
- a storyteller
- a digital operator
- an internal communicator
- an advisor
- a culture shaper
- a visibility architect
- a leader

That evolution is not optional. It is already happening.

Chapter 34
The Future of AEC Belongs to the Brave
Why clarity, courage, and truth-telling will define the next decade

This industry is not just evolving. It is being rewritten.

Digital acceleration.

Younger buyers.

A real talent gap.

Rising expectations.

Increased pressure.

The longest resumes will not shape the next decade. It will be shaped by the people willing to step forward while others hesitate.

Bravery in AEC marketing doesn't look like theatrics. It looks like clarity. It looks like alignment. It looks like truth-telling. It looks like questioning habits that no longer serve the business. It looks like anticipating what's coming instead of defending what's familiar.

Brave marketing leaders say what others won't:

- This process isn't working.
- Our messaging is outdated.

- We're not visible enough.
- Our people are exhausted.
- We have a leadership gap coming.

These aren't criticisms. They're realities. And acknowledging reality is the first act of leadership. You don't need permission to lead. You need courage.

Epilogue
Why Your Work Matters

The AEC industry does more than design buildings. It shapes how people live, learn, heal, work, gather, move, and feel safe. It delivers the systems that make daily life possible—housing, healthcare, infrastructure, justice, education, energy, water, and public space. These aren't abstract outcomes. They are human needs.

And the people who make that happen—planners, architects, engineers, builders—are extraordinarily skilled. They spend years mastering complex disciplines. They learn how to solve problems most people will never fully understand. They carry enormous responsibility, often under intense pressure, with real consequences when things go wrong.

What they are rarely taught is how to *communicate* that expertise. They are trained to design, calculate, coordinate, construct, and deliver. They are not trained to articulate value, frame ideas, shape perception, or guide decision-making outside their discipline.

That gap is not a flaw in the industry. It's the reason your role exists. AEC marketing is not about promotion. It is about translation.

You translate complexity into clarity.

You translate expertise into confidence.

You translate technical brilliance into stories that decision-makers can understand and trust.

Without that translation, great ideas stall. Great teams stay invisible. Great solutions never make it to the table.

You help ensure that the right teams are chosen to design hospitals, schools, cities, campuses, infrastructure, and places that will shape communities for generations. You influence which ideas are funded, which approaches are trusted, and which firms are given the opportunity to solve the problems that matter most.

That is not peripheral work.

That is consequential work.

And it is why AEC marketing, when done well, is one of the most meaningful career paths in professional services.

It allows you to work alongside some of the most intelligent people in the world —not to replace their expertise, but to amplify it. It gives you visibility into how decisions are made, how power moves, how trust forms, and how organizations evolve. It places you in a position to connect dots others don't see—between business strategy and human need, between vision and execution, between ideas and outcomes.

Few roles offer that kind of vantage point.

And when you choose to take it seriously—not as support, not as execution, but as a profession in its own right—you become essential.

Not because you demand it.

But because the industry needs it.

That is why your role matters.

That is why this path is worth choosing.

And that is why the future of the built environment will be shaped not only by those who design and build it—but by those who help the world understand why their work matters.

Acknowledgements

This book exists because of the people who challenged me, trusted me, and pushed me to think more clearly over the course of my career. It also exists because I believe I was called to do this work. There were moments when the path forward was not obvious, when the timing made no sense on paper, and when the risks felt bigger than the rewards. Looking back, I can see God's hand in the doors that opened, the people who showed up at exactly the right time, and the clarity that came when I was willing to trust the process even when I couldn't see the full plan.

First, I want to thank my husband, Randy Sparks, my partner in business and in life. Your belief in me made it possible to begin Smartegies during the height of the Great Recession. I don't know many husbands who would have supported the timing of all of it, but you never doubted my abilities and believed in what I could do, even when I didn't.

To Lamar Wakefield, who allowed me into your organization, your strategy conversations, and your moments of uncertainty, thank you for your trust. As one of my earliest clients, many of the insights in this book were earned through real conversations, real challenges, and real decisions we made together.

To Bobby Brothers, Jim Pustejovsky, Ennis Parker, and Eric Anderson, thank you for teaching me how the AEC industry works, how to think critically, how to lead, and how to challenge the status quo. Much of what I know came from watching you work.

To my parents, thank you for laying the foundation that made everything else possible. You taught me the value of hard work, integrity, independence, and perseverance long before I ever applied those lessons to a career. This gave me the confidence to take risks and trust my instincts. I carry what you taught me into everything I do.

To Katie Cash, thank you for helping turn my dream into something real. I love my job because you have been by my side for most of the journey. This book is stronger because of your courage to tell me the first pass was a B+.

To the marketing professionals, seller doers, and emerging leaders I've had the privilege of coaching and collaborating with, you are the reason I wrote this. Your questions, frustrations, and ambition made it clear that this industry needs new language, new systems, and new leadership.

And finally, to my son, Nathan, thank you for inspiring me to be the best version of myself. Your faith, optimism, and kindness remind me how blessed I am to be your mom.

This book is about the future of an industry. But it was built through relationships and people who have shown me love, support, and honesty. And for that, I am deeply grateful.

About The Author

Judy Sparks is a Fractional CMO, marketing strategist, and trusted advisor to architecture, engineering, construction, and commercial real estate companies across North America. She is the founder and CEO of Smartegies, a consultancy dedicated exclusively to helping firms in the built environment grow with intention, clarity, and confidence.

With more than three decades in the AEC industry, Judy has worked on both sides of the table—as an in-house marketing leader inside large, complex organizations and as a strategic advisor to more than 300 firms ranging from boutique practices to national and international brands. Her work sits at the intersection of marketing, business development, and leadership, helping firms move beyond reactive pursuits and into sustainable, pipeline-driven growth.

Judy is known in the industry for her candid, no-filter perspective on what is—and is not—working in AEC marketing today.

She is the creator of the Scalable 6™ Framework, a proprietary model designed specifically for the built environment that aligns six critical areas of growth: brand, communications, account-based marketing, digital visibility, sales enablement, and talent strategy. The framework is used by firms seeking to scale without building bloated infrastructure or chasing disconnected tactics.

In addition to advising clients, Judy is a sought-after speaker, educator, and coach. She co-developed and co-taught the Construction Marketing curriculum for the Georgia Institute of Technology's School of Building Construction, where she served as a part-time lecturer. Her work focuses on helping marketers think like executives, helping leaders understand modern marketing, and elevating the profession within an industry undergoing rapid change.

Judy lives in Marietta, Georgia, where she continues to write, teach, and advise firms shaping the future of the built environment. *The Modern AEC Marketer* is her first book.

www.ingramcontent.com/pod-product-compliance
Lightning Source LLC
Chambersburg PA
CBHW050901160426
43194CB00011B/2239